LEGAL WRITING

Legal Writing guides students comprehensively through this essential legal skill, and addresses a range of examining methods, from questions to final essays and problem answers. It considers how to deconstruct essay and problem questions and how to conduct and apply legal research to answer set questions.

The book explains how to reference others' work clearly and correctly, and is a useful tool for students concerned about issues of plagiarism. It also focuses on how to develop and communicate legal arguments, and both good and bad examples of written work are considered and discussed.

Legal Writing is principally appropriate to undergraduate students, particularly at the beginning of their degree studies, and to GDL and CPE students.

Accompanied by a new companion website, *Legal Writing* is supported by a variety of online resources, including:

- Multiple choice questions on correct referencing
- An exercise on quoting, paraphrasing and plagiarism
- Commentary on a specimen exam answer
- Revision tips and guidance
- Answers to frequently asked questions relating to all aspects of legal writing

Lisa Webley teaches legal skills, research methods and public law at the University of Westminster, where she is a Reader in Law. She is also a Research Fellow at the Institute of Advanced Legal Studies in London.

www.routledge.com/textbooks/9780415491914

LEGAL
WRITING

second edition

LISA WEBLEY

Routledge·Cavendish
Taylor & Francis Group
LONDON AND NEW YORK

Second edition published 2010
by Routledge-Cavendish
2 Park Square, Milton Park, Abingdon, Oxon, OX14 4RN

Simultaneously published in the USA and Canada
by Routledge-Cavendish
270 Madison Avenue, New York, NY 10016

Routledge-Cavendish is an imprint of the Taylor & Francis Group, an informa business

© 2005, 2010 Lisa Webley

First edition published 2005
by Cavendish Publishing Limited

Typeset in Adobe Garamond by RefineCatch Limited, Bungay, Suffolk
Printed and bound in Great Britain by TJ International, Padstow, Cornwall

British Library Cataloguing in Publication Data
A catalogue record for this book is available from the British Library

Library of Congress Cataloging-in-Publication Data
Webley, Lisa.
   Legal writing / Lisa Webley. – 2nd ed.
      p. cm.
   Includes bibliographical references.
   1. Legal composition.   I. Title.
   KD404.W42 2010
   808′.06634 – dc22

                              2009009482

ISBN10: 0–415–49191–6 (pbk)
ISBN13: 978–0–415–49191–4 (pbk)

ISBN10: 0–203–87688–1 (eBook)
ISBN13: 978–0–203–87688–6 (eBook)

CONTENTS

ACKNOWLEDGEMENTS

I should like to thank, as ever, my parents Jan and Paul Webley and my sister Jemma for their continual patience. I am very grateful for the support of my friends Ruth Baxter and Saran Turnbull, and for my friends and colleagues at work: Liz Duff, Guy Osborn and Stephanie Roberts, and particularly to Steve Greenfield with whom I have taught legal skills for many years. I have learnt a lot from many of the first-year LLB students at the University of Westminster over the years. Some have provided valuable feedback on the first edition. I should also like to thank the Law School for allowing me to make use of adapted versions of some of the materials that Steve Greenfield and I have developed and used on our Legal Skills and Process 1 first-year module. Finally, I should like to thank the anonymous and not so anonymous reviewers who commented on the first edition of this book and provided useful guidance on how to improve it. As ever, all omissions and errors in the book are mine alone. The book remains a work in progress and in the spirit of legal writing, I should be happy to receive feedback on how it may be improved in the future.

AN INTRODUCTION TO LEGAL WRITING

Law degrees involve a lot of written work. Lecturers stress that the manipulation and use of language is at the heart of the common law legal tradition. Students are expected to be able to write in a range of written styles, to a high standard. They are reminded that effective communication is the key to success. And yet, law degrees in the UK, in contrast to their US cousins, rarely focus on writing skills. Traditionally, many academics have expected students to arrive at University with well-formed writing skills, believing that these will have been taught previously at A2 stage and Access Course stage. We are beginning to recognise that this is not always the case. In any event, we can always improve on our written abilities. Academics continue to develop their written skills, as do practitioners. Written skills are not things that you learn once and for all and then continue to put into practice in the same way, year after year. We could all benefit from tips, good practice suggestions and examples of how our writing could be improved. I hope that this book will provide some of those to help you in your writing journey.

Legal writing is something that many of us will do every day, but we rarely receive feedback on our written style unless our work is being formally assessed either by a lecturer or, in the case of an academic, by an academic who is reviewing our work for potential publication. On that basis, in order to improve we need to develop reflexive skills so that we can critique our own work and learn to develop on our own. We also need to maximise the learning opportunity from the few occasions when we do get informal and formal feedback from others on our writing.

Students often tell lecturers that they find the way they are assessed a complete mystery. They explain that they write an essay or an answer to a problem question, but do not really understand what they are supposed to do, how to go about it and what the marks they are awarded really mean about the quality of their answer. It is all just too confusing. A number of factors contribute to a good written answer and we shall address the important ones as we work our way through the book. They include the extent to which the student has:

- understood the task that has been set;

- understood how they will be assessed;

- carried out research of the relevant law;

- taken appropriate notes on relevant legal and related issues;

- identified issues that are relevant to answering the question;

- planned the answer;

- written and presented the issues to answer the question;

- provided evidence in support of the points being made;

- referenced others' work; and

- polished the final draft.

It all sounds terribly hard work and rather complicated. Having said that, some of these writing stages come naturally to each one of us and others can be learnt. This book will take you through each one in turn to help you to improve your written work in law.

Most law students will be asked to write two main types of written work – essay answers and problem question answers. There are other forms of written assessment including reflective essays (which also follow similar patterns to standard essays but require the student to reflect on their own performance, their skills and knowledge), memos and briefing sheets (not dissimilar to problem question answers). Students may also research and write an extended essay or dissertation at some point in their undergraduate or postgraduate studies. Dissertations are essays that include a greater research component, but are more similar to essays in written style than to problem question answers.

Despite the differences between these forms of written work, there are some easy basic rules that work for most forms of written assessment. Writing an essay or giving an answer to a problem question is simply a way to communicate what you think about the issues raised in the title or the scenario in the problem. Written answers such as these demonstrate the weight of evidence that you have in favour of each of the propositions that you raise – in other words the authority of your opinion. The arguments that you make and the evidence that you present feed into the conclusions that you reach. Assessments may feel like impossible feats, but they are really relatively easy as long as you follow a few easy steps and (and this is the hard part) you start to write more than 24 hours before your deadline!

Excellent written work is a culmination of a number of factors coming together. It is a product of a good written style that communicates the ideas in the right way to the relevant audience. Excellent written work focuses on the main issues that have been raised by the question or scenario. It does not end at description, but also provides analysis. Your analysis (your authoritative opinion) needs to be well evidenced with authoritative research that adds credence to what you are saying. It culminates in a well-considered conclusion that sums up the analysis that you have provided, as a final answer to the question. But, it does help for the writer to understand what they are trying to communicate, to what end and to whom.

This chapter will explain the purpose of essays, answers to problem questions and of dissertations. Hopefully that will set you on the right track. After that you may want to follow through the steps in the order presented. You should end up with a reasonable essay or problem answer, if you do. If in doubt, stick with the formula. If you are confident, you may come up with your own; there is no one correct way to go about writing. What follows is simply one view of how to communicate your views effectively; there are others, some of which are discussed in the books listed in the bibliography. You may wish to look at some of those as well to help you.

THE PURPOSE OF AN ESSAY

> **An essay question is a way of examining your understanding and your considered and evidenced views on an area of law, practice or policy. Your answer displays your considered response to a question, which weighs up competing viewpoints. It shows how you reached your conclusions with the evidence that you have drawn upon to come to your final view.**

Your first response to any essay should be to spend some time considering what the question is asking you to do. Essays are assessed against the question that has been set, not against your general knowledge of the subject area (as shown in the specimen assessment criteria in the next chapter). Your diagnosis of the nature of the question will either send you off on the correct path, or will send you off on a wild goose chase. Spend time reading the question and checking that you understand it. Once you are clear on the nature of the question, it is important that you focus on its purpose. Have you been asked to do one of the following things and, if so, are you clear on what that means?

Contrast: This is sometimes written as 'compare and contrast' and is perhaps easy to understand if you substitute the word 'compare' for contrast. You should consider the similarities and differences between the issues set out in the question and provide evidence to back up what you are saying in your essay.

Criticise: Give your views about the issues in the question. You must support your views with evidence from other legal writing. Criticise does not mean that you only write about the negative things that you find during your research. It is really an instruction to you to think critically – to consider the issue in detail and to argue against the proposition in the question, but also to concede when a point made on the positive side is a valid one. Some questions may use the word 'critique' instead, which simply denotes that you should examine the evidence on both sides and offer a thoughtful opinion (analysis) by way of conclusion.

Discuss and/or do you agree? (Often after a quote): The answer to this cannot be just 'yes' or 'no'! Your essay should define the issues in the question and then move on to consider different viewpoints on those issues, or different research evidence on those issues. You may find it helpful to write down the strengths and weaknesses or arguments for and against the proposition mentioned in the quotation. Make sure cases, law and/or other writers support these. You should conclude by giving your considered view on the quotation once you have worked your way through others' views and weighed up the evidence.

Evaluate: Give your opinion on the validity of a statement made or an issue raised in the question in the light of evidence you have to support differing viewpoints from your research/reading.

Explain: What is the significance of whatever was set out in the question? Give a definition of the issues raised in the question, followed by an outline of the nature of the issues and the implications of the issues. You will need to do some research or have done some research in order to answer this type of question properly.

Outline/Summarise: Give the main points in relation to the issue raised in the question, without getting stuck in the detail of the issue. This is similar to providing an overview.

For the most part, all of the instructions set out above are asking you to do some research or reading on the topic in the question, or to have done some before entering the exam room. Such questions aim to require you to apply your knowledge to the question to provide a considered response. An essay may be set to assess your ability to conduct research as well as to assess your understanding and your written skills. If this is the case then leave plenty of time within which to complete the research stage before you begin the writing stage. Chapter 5 provides a brief guide to how to carry out library-based research and how to use your research findings in your writing.

An essay may also have been set to assess your ability to write under timed conditions. If this is the case then you may be expected to carry out research on a given topic prior to the timed essay, to include relevant research findings in a notebook and then to use your research findings under timed conditions to answer a question on the given topic. This type of assessment requires you to conduct your research in detail and to organise your research evidence into a notebook in advance of the day of the timed essay. You may be able to write a good essay under timed conditions, but without the research to back up your points you will not do as well as you would have hoped. You will be expected to provide more evidence in support of your arguments if you are permitted to take materials into an exam room or to write your coursework with access to your notes.

In short, an excellent essay provides a complete answer to the question within the confines of the word limit. It is written in good English, in a style that is appropriate to the intended audience. All points made are backed up with authoritative evidence. Finally, the essay meets any assessment requirements.

THE PURPOSE OF A PROBLEM ANSWER

> A problem question is a scenario that sets out the facts of a given situation. The facts are there to prompt the writer (acting as a barrister) to give a legal opinion to the party or parties, to assist them in deciding what legal action they should take on the basis of the barrister's legal opinion.

A problem question tests your ability to analyse the facts in the scenario and to work out which ones are agreed or accepted by all the parties (different sides) in the scenario, which ones are disputed and must be discussed and which facts are not discussed but may have a bearing on the outcome of the case. Those facts that are important but are not present in the problem question should be mentioned in the answer so that the solicitor, the person to whom you are writing your opinion, may investigate those facts further before proceeding with the case.

A problem question also tests your ability to diagnose the legal issues that are relevant to the parties and to provide a considered response on the likely outcome of each point of law, if they were to be argued in court on the basis of the facts as presented. This is done by arguing the competing precedents and statutory points that relate to the facts in the question. You will need to display your understanding of the law in the area by referring to cases and to statutes and other legislation to back up the general principles of law that you explain to the solicitor representing the party to be advised. You will need to employ your understanding of statutory interpretation for UK legislation and also EU law. You will also need to become adept at applying and distinguishing helpful and unhelpful precedents. To do this you will also need strong research skills so that you are able to find all the relevant authorities.

Your final role in the answer is to explain what the likely outcome of the case would be if it were to proceed to court (or in some instances to another dispute resolution mechanism) and the remedies that the client could hope to obtain. The final conclusion to a problem question answer is usually your assessment of what the client should do in respect of the case – take it to court, settle it out of court or drop the case altogether.

A typical, if complicated, public law problem question would look something like this:

Parliament has introduced a new licensing scheme to make sure that all individuals who want to work as art dealers must hold a licence. Parliament passes the Art Dealers Licensing Act 2008 and the Act states that the new Licensing Authority is responsible for administering the Art Dealers' licensing scheme. Section 2 states that 'The Licensing Authority may issue a licence to an individual to act as an art dealer if the individual has not been convicted of a serious criminal offence and if the individual has a recognised qualification in an art related subject.' The Act further states that a degree in art or art history from a UK university will automatically be recognised for the purposes of the Act. Interim arrangements exist which require current art dealers to apply for a licence within six months of entry into force of the Act.

The following events occur:
Ruth works for an art dealer in London. Ruth is not sure whether she needs a licence as she currently does not sell art, she only values it. She has no criminal convictions and has a degree in art history from a UK university. She applies to the Licensing Authority for a licence, just in case she needs to have one. Her application is refused. The Authority writes to tell her that she must stop her work immediately as she does not have the required qualification and she is not a fit and proper person to be an art dealer. In the letter the Authority tells her that the decision is final and cannot be challenged in any court whatsoever. Ruth telephones the Licensing Authority to see

whether she really needs a licence and speaks to John, the decision-maker. He tells her that he considers that women do not make good art dealers or valuers. Ruth seeks legal advice from you.

The professional publication for art dealers runs an article in their journal about Ruth's situation. A reader of the publication, Phillip, hears of the problem and approaches Ruth to let her know that he would be willing to challenge the decision on her behalf.

Advise Ruth about her case and Phillip's suggestion to her about his role in bringing an action on her behalf.

The problem is typical in that it asks the student to advise some of the people the parties or clients, in the scenario, in this instance Ruth and via Ruth also Phillip. It also gives the student most of the factual information needed to provide an assessment of the likely chances of success or failure in a legal action.

The student's role is that of a barrister, who is providing a legal opinion, pre-trial to the party's solicitor, which the solicitor may share with the client. The opinion should provide the solicitor and client with the information that is needed in order to make a decision on whether they should pursue the action (through negotiation, mediation, arbitration or the courts, as appropriate) or whether they should drop the case as it is unlikely to succeed. The student is not acting as an advocate for the purposes of this exercise. This is very important. If the student were acting as an advocate, as in a moot exchange, for example, then s/he would be trying to make the best case possible for Ruth to the judge. The student would be downplaying any inconvenient legal points and evidence that the other side may rely on. In this instance, the student provides an unvarnished account to allow the client to decide what steps to take next. It is important to present the information for and against Ruth's case, to permit her to make an informed choice.

Chapter 3 will provide a structure you may follow to assist you in answering problem questions. It will take you through the process, step-by-step, and suggest ways in which you may phrase your answer.

THE PURPOSE OF AN EXTENDED RESEARCH ESSAY OR DISSERTATION

1 A dissertation is an extended piece of writing that is the culmination of in-depth research.

2 It is usual for the student to set the question, rather than to research and write a dissertation to a preset question.

3 The dissertation takes the reader through the relevant issues, providing research evidence to back up competing viewpoints and providing a final answer to the question.

4 It is similar to an essay in nature, but usually requires more detailed research and a longer discussion of the issues.

A dissertation is an extended piece of writing – often 8,000–10,000 words long at undergraduate level, 10,000 words or more at postgraduate level – which allows a student to explore an area of interest to them and to write an answer to a question that the student has posed. It is not a collection of information on a topic, but it is a form of extended essay. Many books have been written on how to research and write dissertations and you may wish to refer to some of these if you are engaged in dissertation research. Chapter 4 considers how to approach, structure and write an extended research essay or dissertation, but does not consider the research process in any detail. A dissertation will require far more in-depth research than would a standard essay, but a student would normally still follow the writing and referencing conventions for other forms of legal writing. In addition, dissertation students tend to be more focused in their writing if they have set themselves a question prior to carrying out the main phase of their research. This is discussed further in Chapter 4.

Hopefully you understand the purpose of essays, problem question answers and dissertations. The next stage is to understand how you will be marked for them. The next chapter will explain the criteria that may be used to assess and grade your work. After that, we move on to specific types of written work, before turning our attention to how to undertake the research required to provide evidence to back up the points that you make. You will also need to reference this evidence correctly, to give appropriate credit to the sources of the evidence, but also to demonstrate that you have thoroughly researched the area. Once your written work is completed in draft, it will need to be finished and polished. There is a chapter on preparation for exams, which often come towards the end of the academic year, after coursework has been completed. Finally, we consider what you should take from the mark and feedback that you have received. It is important to learn what you can from your past performance to develop your potential for future written work, legal scholarship and legal practice. An important part of being a professional is reflective practice.

1

HOW TO DO WELL IN ASSESSMENTS

Students tend to focus on assessments rather than on the extent to which they are developing their knowledge of law and their ability to communicate that knowledge in writing (and orally). This tends to frustrate academics, who do not feel that assessments are the 'be all and end all' of the learning experience at university. However, students' preoccupation with assessments is understandable, as it is the assessments that determine the degree classification you will achieve. Related to this, once out of university an employer may ask first what grades you got before discussing the skills and attributes you have as a person. By looking at the way you will be assessed by your lecturer, you should be able to improve your performance and concentrate a little more on what you are learning rather than on how you are being tested. It is less of a mystery than you think. This chapter will take you through an example of assessment and grading criteria that may be similar to the ones that will be used to assess your work, to help you to understand what lecturers are looking for.

It is important to bear in mind that assessments are a way of indicating your current level of knowledge and skill. They are not an end in themselves, but a way for you to see how far along the learning journey you have come, and the direction you need to take for the next phase. Completing the assessment is a major hurdle, but it is only the first of many. After that, you need to take the time to assess how well you have demonstrated your knowledge and skill levels and make adjustments to your assessment to improve your chances of success. Once you receive your feedback, you embark upon the next stage of development, that is, to take the positive and negative comments (and the mark) as guidance for what you need to do to improve your skills and your legal knowledge. These stages form part of a continuous learning cycle. We shall begin right at the beginning, with the need to start with a clear idea.

1.1: STARTING OUT WITH A CLEAR IDEA

To maximise your chances of achieving a good mark in an assessed piece of work, you should have:

1 **An understanding of the specific task that has been set (from the question and/or instructions for the assessment);**

2 **An understanding of how the written work will be assessed (assessment criteria);**

3 **An understanding of how the written work will be graded (grading criteria).**

This chapter will take you through these stages – the way in which you are likely to be assessed and how to maximise your chances of achieving good marks at this stage of writing your answer. It may be helpful to think of it in these terms. If you were an advocate and you were about to go into court to represent a client in a serious criminal case, you would want to know a little about the way in which the court process will work and the way that the judge and the jury will decide upon your client's fate, in order to know how best to prepare your case. You would not go in to court without an understanding of how the case will be decided and how your presentation is likely to be judged. Similarly, you would not embark upon an assessment without understanding how you were to be assessed.

How you will be assessed is a clue to how to answer the essay or problem question.

Most courses have published assessment criteria and, if they are not in your course or module handbook, then try to get hold of a copy of them from your lecturer. The criteria are really the key to understanding how you need to approach the task set. They are also the key to knowing what skill and knowledge requirements are expected of you at your level of study. They provide a benchmark against which you may measure yourself. An example of assessment criteria at level 4 (first-year undergraduate level) is as follows:[1]

---

1 These are generic assessment criteria adapted from those used by the University of Westminster LLB for public law level 4 assessments (1st year undergraduate).

> **Assessment criteria for coursework assessed by essay**
>
> In this assessment the student should write an essay plan and an essay in answer to the question.
>
> In the essay students should:
>
> - address the question asked;
>
> - identify the relevant areas with precision;
>
> - demonstrate a thorough knowledge and understanding of the relevant principles, including an analysis of them;
>
> - show evidence of research and reading;
>
> - present a coherent argument for the position taken;
>
> - present work that is well written and structured;
>
> - correctly reference others' work where used.
>
> In the essay plan students should:
>
> - show evidence of having dissected the question;
>
> - show evidence of having identified relevant issues;
>
> - provide headings to indicate the content of each paragraph;
>
> - indicate relevant material under paragraph headings;
>
> - provide a structure for the essay.

The assessment criteria make it clear that for this assessment there are two parts to the written phase of this assessment – an essay plan and an essay – and that both parts have their own assessment criteria. The criteria demonstrate that the marker is looking for different things from the two parts. It is important that the criteria are met for each. They are testing your ability to use different skills. To achieve a good mark in this assessment a student would have to write an essay plan that is split into sections indicating the content of each paragraph. The plan should show that the student has read the question and dissected it so that s/he can understand and answer it. The essay is a continuation of the plan; in other words it follows the plan but is written in full sentences and paragraphs rather than in note form. The essay should address the question posed, and it should demonstrate that the student has understood the principles relevant to the question and has constructed arguments and cited evidence to back up arguments

3

relevant to answering the question. This evidence is a product of research carried out by the student prior to writing the essay.

The assessment criteria for the exam assessment are slightly different again. In this example students must answer three questions from a paper containing six questions made up of a mix of essay questions and problem questions. Students are assessed against the following:

Assessment criteria for exam written answers[2]

A student should:

- identify relevant issues and principles in respect of the question;

- demonstrate knowledge of the relevant principles and give examples where appropriate;

- attempt to apply the principles in their answer;

- demonstrate an understanding of and answer the question;

- apply statutory and judicial material in any hypothetical factual situations;

- demonstrate an ability to answer questions in exam conditions with appropriate regard to timing;

- communicate in good English.

The criteria are similar to those for the coursework, but they are set slightly differently. Essays and problem questions written in closed book exams (exams in which you are not permitted to refer to any materials in the exam room) are a test of knowledge and the ability to apply that knowledge to answer the question, rather than such a test of a student's research ability. Students need to be clear about the general principles of law in a given area and the evidence that supports those general principles prior to entering the exam. Once in the exam, a student would need to dissect the question, plan an answer and apply the general principles. Exam technique is discussed in more detail in Chapter 8; however, the important point here is to be sure about how you will be assessed prior to embarking upon the assessed task.

Your essay or problem question answer, or plan, will be read in the light of the criteria and how you do will depend on how far you have met the criteria. Many courses also have grading criteria, which the marker will use in

---

2 Once again, these criteria are adapted from those used in LLB public law level 4 exams at the University of Westminster.

conjunction with the assessment criteria to work out your mark. Grading criteria do vary, so be sure to check the grading criteria that are used in your law school. Two examples are provided by the Higher Education Funding Council for England (HEFCE) through an authoritative document known as the QAA Benchmark Statements for Law. This document is a point of reference for law schools, and so although criteria may vary from institution to institution, it is likely that most law schools will be looking for similar levels of attainment at each of the grade boundaries. In this chapter we focus on the example of grading criteria set out in Appendix C, which are considered to be an example of good practice in a legal context by the QAA. Each band of grading criteria sets out the minimum levels of attainment that a student will have achieved at the point when they graduate from a law honours degree (usually a LLB degree, but it could be a Graduate Diploma/CPE programme too). Many institutions will expect a lesser standard at level 4 (first year) and level 5 (second year) than they do at level 6 (third and usually graduating year). Consequently the QAA criteria may be set a little higher than those that are being used in your institution in your first and second year of studies. However, it is important to aim high at level 4 so that you have a good grasp of the basic skills that you need in order to excel in your level 5 and 6 years. This allows you to spend more time on honing your skills and also on conducting detailed research and critical analysis that should result in you achieving high marks. It is better to learn the skills as soon as possible, so that you may concentrate on perfecting them while conducting detailed research and excellent written work for your other assessments.

A third class answer at level 6, one that falls into the 40–49% boundary will have been assessed as set out in the box below.

3rd (40–49%)

This assessment will demonstrate a basic understanding of the main issues but not coherently or correctly presented.

Third class answers demonstrate some knowledge or understanding of the general area but a third class answer tends to be weak in the following ways:

- descriptive only;

- does not answer the question directly;

- misses key points;

- contains important inaccuracies;

- covers material sparsely, possibly in note form;

- assertions not supported by authority or evidence.

A student will achieve a mark of 40–49% if s/he identifies the subject area that the question addresses and writes something that is relevant to the question. The assessment will also meet the minimum standards of presentation. It will demonstrate that the student is familiar with the subject area. A student who achieves a third class mark has missed key points raised by the question, and his or her answer may also contain some important inaccuracies. There is a real lack of evidence in support of the points being made. The assessment is also largely descriptive, meaning that the student has simply repeated what someone else has said or written, rather than thinking about what this means and providing his or her own thoughts (analysis). This would be similar to being an advocate for the defence in a murder case, to stand before the jury and to explain a little bit about the history of the law of murder, before sitting back down again. The jury would be none the wiser about whether or not the defendant had anything to do with the murder and the barrister would not have presented evidence to them to help them to make up their own minds. A written answer along these lines would be fairly basic and would benefit from a clearer understanding of what the question was asking. A student with a mark at this level should concentrate on the first essay writing stage set out in the next chapter – considering the nature of the question, before starting the research and writing phases.

A student will achieve a 2.2 mark for his or her assessment if the written work is judged to meet the following criteria.

2:2 (50–59%)

This assessment provides a substantially correct answer, which shows an understanding of the basic principles.

Lower second class answers display an acceptable level of competence, as indicated by the following qualities:

- generally accurate;

- providing an adequate answer to the question based largely on textbooks and lecture notes;

- clearly presented;

- no real development of arguments;

- may contain some major error or omission;

- a lower second class answer may also be a good answer (i.e. an upper second class answer) to a related question but not one set by the examiner.

A student will achieve a mark of 50–59% if s/he correctly identifies the subject area of the question (as for an essay of 40–49%) but then goes on to discuss the main issue raised in the question as well as some related issues along with some relevant cases, statutes or academic opinion. The cases, statutes or academic opinion (which shows some evidence of reading or research) will have been applied to the question or the facts of the problem question in some way. However, there will not be evidence of extensive research. A student will have constructed an argument and shown an adequate understanding of the subject area, but without sufficient focus on the question. Students who achieve a mark of 50–59% should concentrate on identifying the issues relevant to the question and using their research findings to construct an argument to answer the question. This is discussed more in the next chapter.

2:1 (60–69%)

An upper second class answer generally shows a sound understanding of both the basic principles and relevant details of the law, supported by examples that are demonstrably well understood and which are presented in a coherent and logical fashion.

The answer should be well presented, display some analytical ability and contain no major errors or omissions. Not necessarily excellent in any area.

Upper second class answers cover a wider band of students. Such answers are clearly highly competent and typically possess the following qualities:

- generally accurate and well-informed;

- reasonably comprehensive;

- well-organised and structured;

- provide evidence of general reading;

- demonstrating a sound grasp of basic principles;

- demonstrating a good understanding of the relevant details;

- succinctly and cogently presented;

- displaying some evidence of insight.

One essential aspect of an upper second class answer is that it must have competently dealt with the question asked by the examiner.

A student who achieves a mark of 60–69% has correctly identified the subject of the question and has also identified most of the relevant issues. In addition, s/he has also cited most of the relevant material that is the subject of the question, having constructed arguments and provided a judgement on differing viewpoints. A student who has achieved a mark in this classification will have demonstrated a good understanding of the subject area, and will have applied that knowledge to the question posed. S/he will also have provided an appropriate conclusion to the question or scenario. A student who wishes to improve should concentrate on developing his or her analysis of each issue by adding a sentence at the end of each paragraph stating why and how the issue is relevant to the question as well as deepening his or her understanding of the subject area by undertaking further reading. This is discussed in more detail in the forthcoming chapters.

1st (70%+)

A first class answer has a thoughtful structure, a clear message displaying personal reflection informed by wider reading of articles and/or other commentaries and a good grasp of detail (as evidenced by the choice of relevant examples which are well integrated into the answer's structure). Complete with no errors or omissions.

First class answers are ones that are exceptionally good for an undergraduate and which excel in at least one and probably several of the following criteria:

- comprehensiveness and accuracy;

- clarity of argument and expression;

- integration of a range of materials;

- evidence of wider reading;

- insight into the theoretical issues.

Excellence in one or more of these areas should be in addition to the qualities expected of an upper second class answer. Although there is no expectation of originality of exposition or treatment, a first class answer is generally expected to spot points rarely seen. A high first (75+%) is expected to display originality and excel in most if not all the aforementioned criteria.

As shown above, a first class answer has to demonstrate a very high level of knowledge and skill, but it is possible to achieve if a student really understands a topic, has conducted in-depth research on the topic and has properly dissected the question and written to it. The criteria indicate that a student is not expected to come up with a new legal theory or to find a completely different way of looking at the law. However, the essay does need to be focused to answer the question, with evidence to back up all the points being made within it. It also needs to be comprehensive and extremely well written.

Not all criteria will necessary apply equally in every type of coursework or examination or with equal weight; for example, in a written examination the evidence of independent research required may be less than in a coursework. Your course will have slightly different criteria and you should check what these are if you are unsure of how you will be graded, or if you do not understand why you have received the mark you have been given for an assessed essay or problem question answer. You should attempt to aim as high as possible, rather than aiming at a bare pass. It sounds obvious, but it is surprising how many students aim at the pass rather than at the higher end of the marking spectrum! Apart from anything else, on a law programme you will use the same skills over and over again. The sooner that you learn how to make good use of the key legal writing and research skills, the more you will get out of your law degree experience. This is likely to mean that you will also enjoy your time on the course rather more too. Plus, the sooner you learn the skills that you need, the more time you can spend on focusing on the detail of each assessment rather than the basics.

As you will have seen from the criteria, the next important stage in the writing process is to dissect the question or problem question scenario to make sure that you have identified the task that has been set for you. If you are writing a dissertation and must formulate a question of your own, follow this stage once you have developed your question with the help of your supervisor. More information is give on formulating questions for dissertations in Chapter 4. The research phase, including reading your lecture and tutorial notes, should focus on the question rather than the topic in general terms. By focusing on the question you give yourself the best chance of achieving the highest mark possible. This is discussed further in the next chapter.

Next steps:

- **You may wish to look back through any previous assessed written work that you have done on your law course. Look at the mark and the comments that you received and consider what we have covered in this chapter. Do you understand why you got the mark that you got? Can you see what you would need to do to improve?**

- You may also wish to read through the example essay provided below and grade it in the light of what you have learnt in this chapter. You may compare your thoughts against the mark and comments given to the work, towards the back of the book.

- Finally, you may wish to examine the assessment criteria and the grading criteria that will be used to assess you for your next piece of coursework (or exam). This should help you to prepare for the assessment, to develop your legal and transferable skills, and to maximise your chances of success.

1.2: APPLY YOUR KNOWLEDGE OF ASSESSMENT CRITERIA

Read through the brief essay below and consider what mark you would give to it, based on the limitation that the essay should be about 500 words in length. Refer back to the assessment criteria and then set out your reasons for giving the mark you have awarded. Check the mark you have awarded and your reasons for the mark against the ones given in the answers section towards the back of the book.

'The British Parliament was once supreme.' Discuss with reference to Britain's membership of the EU and its obligations in relation to the European Convention on Human Rights.

This issue of parliamentary sovereignty has been that Parliament has been sovereign throughout centuries until the UK joined the European Community (European Communities Act 1972). Theorists such as Dicey have argued that Parliament is so powerful and so totally sovereign that it is allowed to do anything that it wishes, even to order that smoking on the streets of Paris could be outlawed by the UK Parliament. However, there are those who disagree with this and the essay will consider opinions for and against whether Parliament is supreme or not.

It may be considered that sovereignty has been lost from Parliament. This is because Britain joined Europe and Europe's power overtook the power of the British Parliament. This was done through the enactment of the ECA 1972. Many are of the belief that the Act is now entrenched, that Parliament cannot repeal it. There was a recent case about this where a man wanted to weigh his fruit and vegetables in pounds and was told he could not because Europe says that we must all use kilogrammes and grammes. This shows that Parliament is no longer supreme.

However, there is a dispute about this point. The case of British Railways Board v. Pickin demonstrates that no Act of Parliament can be held to be invalid. This suggests that the courts must apply a British Act of Parliament and that Parliament can enact any law that it wishes; as long as the Act is passed it will become law in this country.

However, the Factortame case in the 1990s shows another side to this situation as the British courts did not apply the British Act of Parliament – the Merchant Shipping Act – but they applied the European law instead as they had been told they must by the European Court of Justice.

Theorists such as Dicey consider Parliament to be supreme. The European Convention on Human Rights now means that Parliament cannot pass any law that is against the Human Rights Act and so this means that Parliament is no longer supreme. However, Parliament was the body that enacted the Human Rights Act and it can repeal the Act and so Parliament is still supreme in the sense that it has only temporarily limited its power.

In conclusion, parliamentary sovereignty may exist as Parliament can repeal the ECA 1972 and the HRA 1998, but the power of Parliament to legislate has been limited by joining Europe and the ECHR and therefore Dicey's theory of sovereignty is not totally correct.

[418 words]

SUMMARY

To maximise your chances of achieving a good mark in an assessed piece of work, you should:

Have an understanding of the specific task that has been set (from the question and/or instructions for the assessment)

Have read through the instructions given with the assessment and be clear on them

Have made sure you have all the information you need about the assessment format, regulations and deadlines

Have an understanding of how the written work will be assessed, having read through the assessment criteria

Have an understanding of how the written work will be graded, having read through the grading criteria

Once you are clear on the task that has been set you may move on to the next phase, as set out in Chapters 2, 3 and 4

2   ESSAY WRITING

It is hard to know where to start when it comes to writing an essay or an answer to a problem question. Students often say that the most difficult stage of writing is to begin, and many academics find this as well with their own writing. When one has lots of ideas, it is difficult to sift through what should be left out and what should be included, and how to put those ideas down on paper. The easiest way is to split the process up into stages and to work through each one in turn without worrying about the next until you have completed the last one. This chapter will consider how to approach writing an essay.

2.1: STAGE 1: READ THE QUESTION

- You are marked on how well you have answered the question.

- Make sure you know what task you have been set.

- You need to spend some time working out what the question is asking you to do.

You should never begin to write until you understand the task that you have been set. Writing in a state of confusion will lead to a confused piece of writing and a lower mark than you would hope to achieve. One way to make sure that you are clear on what the question is asking you to do is to rewrite the question in different words, or to write out the main subject of the question followed by the specific points you must address in order to answer the question fully. You may need to expand on the title in order to make sense of it. A typical essay title would be something like this:

'The British Parliament was once supreme.' Discuss with reference to Britain's membership of the EU and its obligations in relation to the European Convention on Human Rights (ECHR).

The essay is asking you to address a number of issues. The main subject of the question is parliamentary supremacy (sometimes known as 'sovereignty' as indicated in the quotation). This should be the subject of your essay. The essay question asks you to discuss parliamentary supremacy, but it also instructs you to consider two issues in particular in your discussion: Britain's membership of the EU and its obligations in relation to the ECHR. Your answer must consider these issues in the light of parliamentary supremacy. It is important that you focus on these issues. Look up any words in the question of which you are unsure, to make sure you are clear before you dissect the question as below. Each word will be in the question for a reason.

So, the question looks something like this, when split up into its constituent parts:

It is important to bear in mind that not every question has a cut and dried answer. Some questions are truly arguable, and open to a variety of different interpretations and answers. These tend to provide some students with the opportunity to show off their abilities, but they may also trip up some students too. They should be approached in similar ways to standard questions but need to be dissected with great care so that you do not wander off the point. You are ready to move on to the next stage of writing once you are clear about the task you have been set.

2.2: STAGE 2: READ THROUGH YOUR NOTES AND MAKE A LIST OF RELEVANT ISSUES

> **Read through any lecture or tutorial notes on the topic. Make a list of issues from your notes that appear to relate to the question.**
>
> **Research the main issues for the subject area and take notes from your textbook, if you have not read around the area already.**
>
> **Carry out further research: you need to look at more than the textbook and the case book to write a good essay.**
>
> - **You should consider other books, journal articles and official publications.**
>
> - **The reading list in the module handbook will give you some ideas of what reading you need to do and where to look for evidence.**
>
> **See Chapter 5 for tips on how to make the most of your reading and how to use research material in your written work.**
>
> **Refer back to the question frequently during your reading, to make sure that you remain focused on it.**

You need to work out which issues are relevant to your question. It is a tricky stage to explain, as the issues are specific to the title that has been set, which does not help you in the early stages of your own writing. Having said that, there are hints to relevant issues and these should be set out in your lectures on the topic that forms the subject of the assessment. Similarly, it is likely that the key issues on a given topic have been discussed in your tutorial or seminar on the area. Finally, the key issues will be set out in your textbook reading, which may have been set as pre-reading for your tutorial. Key issues are principles or concepts; they are not details or reams of facts. Key issues would include the general principles of offer and acceptance in contract law, or principles that must be demonstrated in order to prove negligence in tort law. In relation to the question above, they will be the theories of parliamentary supremacy in public law and how the established theories of supremacy have been affected by membership of the EU or signature of the ECHR. Cases, statutes and the detail of individual theories are all evidence of the key principles or concepts rather than the principles or concepts themselves.

You should take notes on the key principles and concepts that form the basis of the question topic, but only include enough information so that you are able to understand the principle along with any evidence that supports differing views of that principle. Try to avoid including lots of other information, as this will simply confuse the issue when you come to plan and to write your essay. In note terms, less may very well mean more marks. Please also make sure that you are clear on whether you are summarising others' words (paraphrasing) or quoting their words directly. You will need to keep a note of the full citation (see Chapter 6 for details) including that page number from which you have found the ideas or the words that you are noting down. This is important, because when you come to reread your notes and begin to write you must be able to distinguish between your ideas, your words and others' ideas and others' words.

When taking notes be sure to either:

- **quote directly from the text that you are reading. Use quotation marks, note down the full citation for the quote including page numbers; or**

- **properly summarise the ideas that you have read in the text, taking a note of the full citation including the page number.**

It is much easier to write a proper summary, if you read and reread the paragraph or phrase and then put the text to one side and think about how you would explain the idea in your own words. You should not use the author's original phrase or make a few word changes as this is not a proper paraphrase, but instead a poor quote. You must make a distinction between explaining others' ideas in your own words, and using others' words in quotation format.

2.3: STAGE 3: ORGANISE YOUR IDEAS INTO A LOGICAL ORDER

- **This is a form of essay plan.**

- **List the issues and number each one.**

- **Write a sentence next to each issue to explain what the issue is.**

- **Note down any evidence you will use to support your discussion of the issue (cases, quotes, etc.) under each issue.**

- **Check that the issues are in a logical order.**

There are many different ways of organising your ideas. Some people draw mind-maps or other forms of diagrams. Others jot down ideas in no particular order, and then rearrange them over time. However, some people prefer a structured text-based approach that they can follow until they come up with a personalised way of organising their material. This is one suggestion as to how to do this. You could make a list of issues that you will discuss in your essay from your notes, but these will be in no particular order. The easiest way to sort them out is to leave then in a list for now (with large gaps in between each issue) and to write a sentence after each issue that explains what the issue is about, like so:

'The British Parliament was once supreme.' Discuss with reference to Britain's membership of the EU and its obligations in relation to the European Convention on Human Rights.

1 **Introduction**

2 **Basic definition of parliamentary supremacy** – This is the term given to a collection of theories that explain that the British Parliament has the supreme power to legislate, to amend and to repeal law in the country.

3 **Theories of parliamentary supremacy** – The differing theories of supremacy suggest that Parliament has different roles and different levels of power to legislate depending on the theorist's view of Parliament.

4 **Parliamentary supremacy and the EU: Parliament is no longer supreme** – There is evidence to suggest that as a result of Britain's membership of the EU, Parliament is no longer supreme.

5 **Parliamentary supremacy and the EU: Parliament remains supreme** – There is evidence to suggest that as a result of Britain's membership of the EU, Parliament remains supreme.

6 **Parliamentary supremacy and the ECHR: Parliament is no longer supreme** – There is evidence to suggest that Parliament lost its supremacy once Britain signed the ECHR.

7 **Parliamentary supremacy and the ECHR: Parliament remains supreme** – There is evidence to suggest that Parliament is still supreme even after Britain signed the ECHR.

8 **Conclusion**

The next stage is to list any evidence you have that relates to the issues – a case, a statutory reference, a quotation or an idea from an academic work. If these point in different directions then group the ones that support a view of that issue and those that are against a view of that issue. For example, for point 4 on the list:

> **4 Parliamentary supremacy and the EU: Parliament is no longer supreme** – There is evidence to suggest that as a result of Britain's membership of the EU, Parliament is no longer supreme.
>
> European Communities Act 1972 [see notes].
>
> Discussion of *Factortame* case on the hierarchy of UK and EU law [see notes].
>
> Reference to Hilaire Barnett's book *Constitutional and Administrative Law* on this point [see notes].

Then write a sentence at the bottom of that issue heading, stating how you think this issue may be relevant to the question, or what it means as regards the question. For example:

> **4 Parliamentary supremacy and the EU: Parliament is no longer supreme** – There is evidence to suggest that as a result of Britain's membership of the EU, Parliament is no longer supreme.
>
> European Communities Act 1972 [see notes].
>
> Discussion of *Factortame* case on the hierarchy of UK and EU law [see notes].
>
> Reference to Hilaire Barnett's book *Constitutional and Administrative Law* [see notes] on this point.
>
> This indicates that where there is a direct conflict between British law and European law then European law will prevail, thus suggesting that the British Parliament is no longer supreme, as European law is hierarchically superior.

Remember to remind yourself of the question at regular intervals to ensure that you are not wandering off the point. Also, consider whether you need to conduct more research so as to deepen your evidence base (see Chapter 5 for more details, if you are unsure) and to provide a more sophisticated analysis. Analysis is simply your assessment of any given issue (your opinion, to an extent), but it must be based on sound evidence. Consequently, if you are making a point and yet you have little (authoritative) evidence in support of the point that you are making, then you will need to conduct more research. Your research and your assessment of what that means, is the key to strong analysis.

Continue with the planning process until you have exhausted all the issues on your list. You should now have a whole series of issues with a sentence explaining each issue, evidence that you could use in a discussion of the issue and a sentence explaining each issue's relevance to the question. Read through your plan and consider whether any of the issues need to be reordered to assist the flow of your ideas. Do some follow on from others? Are some totally unconnected and need to be kept separate? Once you are happy with the order then you are ready to move on to the writing stage of your essay or to your problem question answer.

2.3.1 START WRITING: YOU ARE NOW READY TO BEGIN TO WRITE

You are only now ready to begin to write your essay or problem question answer. It is important that you have first completed the writing stages above, as otherwise you are likely to jump in to the middle of the essay and then write around in circles, with no clear idea of what you need to say and how you will attempt to say it. The writing process can be split into small and manageable steps. Good luck with your writing!

2.4: STAGE 4: WRITING YOUR INTRODUCTION

I have put this section here, as many people believe that you should start at the beginning and write your introduction first. However, many of us find this difficult and in fact leave the introduction to the end of our writing process. We shall consider it here, but please bear in mind that you may find it easier to write your introduction (or at least rewrite your introduction) once you have reviewed the first draft of your essay.

> Set out your approach to answering the question by mentioning briefly the issues you will cover.
>
> If you really cannot do this then you may not be that clear on how you are going to approach answering the question. Go back to the question to check that you understand the task that you have been set.

Your introduction may now be relatively easy to write as your introduction is simply a paragraph in which you set out the task that you have been set (very briefly) and you explain the issues that you will deal with in your essay or problem question answer. You should be able to do this from the plan that you developed at stage three above. A simple introduction may look something like this:

> It has been suggested that the British Parliament was once supreme, but that its supremacy has been eroded as a result of Britain's membership of the EU and its signature of the European Convention on Human Rights. In order to examine this proposition it is necessary to consider the definition of parliamentary supremacy and differing theories of supremacy. The essay will consider evidence in respect of Britain's membership of the EU and the extent to which that affects Parliamentary supremacy. The essay will also consider Britain's signature of the European Convention of Human Rights in the same light.

The first sentence sets out the purpose of the essay

The next three sentences set out the issues to be addressed in order to fulfil the task

However, as mentioned previously, some people find it much easier to write their introduction towards the end of the writing process, usually once they have a first draft of the main body of the essay. This is because some people make connections between issues and come up with ideas as they are writing. Consider how you understand what it is that you know. Do you make connections and come to answers through talking to people, drawing diagrams or writing text? If the latter, then you may want to postpone your introduction until you have had a first go at writing the essay. But, if you prefer to talk through your ideas, or to draw diagrams as an initial step, then you may prefer to begin at the beginning and write your introduction as a first stage.

2.5: STAGE 5: WRITING THE MIDDLE SECTION OF YOUR ESSAY

- **Organise your ideas into paragraphs. One paragraph should contain one issue.**

- **At the beginning of each paragraph state what the issue is.**

- **Develop and discuss the issue within the middle part of the paragraph.**

- Provide authoritative evidence for the points you are making.

- Finish the paragraph by stating why this issue is relevant to answering the question.

The middle section of your essay is made up of a series of paragraphs and each paragraph will correspond to one of the issues that you have set out in your plan at stage three above. The middle section of your essay will also be relatively straightforward to write from your plan, if you have followed the stages through in order.

2.5.1 WHAT IS A PARAGRAPH?

A paragraph is a block of text. Some people indent the first line so that it starts slightly further along the page than the rest of the lines in that block of text. Other people prefer to stick to a block of text that begins at the same point on each line, just as this one does. This is increasingly common as people use word processors to write their assessments. If you are unsure about what is accepted practice in your law school, check with your tutor to see if there are guidelines on presentation of work. A paragraph should be a self-contained unit, which means that you should finish off your idea or issue in one block of text before moving on to another. If the paragraph looks to be rather long, then consider whether you have more than one idea or one issue in that one paragraph and split it accordingly.

2.5.2 HOW DO I CONSTRUCT MY PARAGRAPH?

The easiest way to write a paragraph is to stick to an easy formula until you feel comfortable with developing a more personalised style of writing. A formula that appears to work for students is set out in stage five. The first sentence of your paragraph sets out the issue that you will write about in the paragraph. This is likely to be similar to the sentence that you have written in your plan next to the listed issue. This sentence explains the content of the paragraph to the reader, so that the reader knows where they are being taken next. The middle part of a paragraph is the discussion section. The sentences in this part will explain the issue by providing the principles associated with the issue and it will set out any evidence to support these principles. If the issue is relatively uncomplicated, you may be able to put arguments for and against the issue in one paragraph. However, if your paragraph looks to be becoming too long, you may wish to split the issue into two paragraphs – one that provides the discussion of the arguments on one side, and one that provides the discussion of the arguments on the other. Your paragraph should be rounded off with one or two concluding sentences, which are very important. The concluding sentence explains how and why the issue is important in relation to the question. This sentence is an important one as it is your original material. You have worked out why it is an important point and your analysis, if well founded, should improve your marks as indicated by the assessment criteria in the introduction to this book. Analysis is simply your own understanding, or assessment, formed as a result of reviewing authoritative evidence. This is why the research process is such an important one, as your analysis is heavily dependent on the material that you have read and considered, and then converted into analysis by applying your new understanding to the question or sub-question.

An example of a well-written paragraph for point four is as follows:

There is evidence to suggest that as a result of Britain's membership of the EU, Parliament is no longer supreme. Britain joined the European Community and, by passing the European Communities Act 1972, gave effect to EC law within our domestic jurisdiction. Section 2(1) states that 'All such rights, powers, liabilities, obligations and restrictions from time to time created or arising by or under the Treaties . . . are without further enactment to be given legal effect or used in the United Kingdom shall be recognised and available in law, and be enforced . . .' This primacy of European Community law was evidenced in the case of *R v. Secretary of State for Transport ex p. Factortame (No. 2)* (1991) in which EC law was applied in that case even though this meant that certain provisions of the Merchant Shipping Act 1988 had to be disapplied as they directly contradicted the EC law.[1] Parliament had passed the Act subsequent to the European legislation and thus there could be no question that the will of Parliament was to legislate in contravention of Community law. This suggests that Parliamentary supremacy has been eroded as the courts will not apply British law that contravenes EC law that is directly applicable in the UK.

This is the first sentence from the original plan

This introduces the pertinent legal issue

Provides detail and evidence of the issues

Explains the primacy of EC law and provides an authoritative case to evidence this point

Explains what this means in relation to the main subject of the question: parliamentary supremacy

Concludes the point by explaining its relevance in regard to the question

---

1 Barnett, H. *Constitutional and Administrative Law* 7th edn. (London: Routledge-Cavendish, 2008) p. 200.

An example of a less well-written and well-considered paragraph making use of similar material would be as follows:

> **The UK Parliament is no longer supreme. The case of *Factortame* tells us that EC law overrides UK law.[2] This case was about Spanish fishermen wanting to fish in British waters using British fishing quotas. The UK courts ruled that they could not as it was against a piece of UK law that required them to register in the UK in order for them to be able to fish here. But the ECJ ruled that they could as EC law is superior to UK law. This shows that parliamentary supremacy no longer exists where EC law applies.**

This paragraph uses substantially the same basic material to the paragraph above and does introduce the idea to be discussed and provide a conclusion that explains how this paragraph assists in answering the question. So far, it is not too bad. However, the relevant statute is not mentioned nor the provisions quoted or summarised. Instead, there is only vague reference to the legal provision. The facts of the case are (not terribly effectively) summarised and there is an attempt to explain the important legal principle established by the case of *Factortame (No. 2)*, but the point is not made crisply. The case reference is not complete and importantly, the (No. 2) is missed so we are unclear which of the five *Factortame* cases is being referred to. This is not a terrible paragraph, as its basic anatomy is relatively sound, but it fails to make the best use of the evidence that it seeks to present. And it does not communicate the point as clearly as it could.

Once you have provided your analysis you may move on to the next paragraph, which should contain the next issue from your essay plan devised in stage three. Repeat the pattern until you have exhausted all the issues on your list.

2.6: WHY USE EVIDENCE?

- Evidence adds weight to your arguments. It shows how you know that what you are saying is valid.

- Evidence helps the reader to consider the authority of your points. If you have good evidence in support of what you are saying, that

---

2 Lecture Notes Membership of EU & Parliamentary Supremacy Nov. 2008.

> suggests authority. If your evidence is sparse or of poor quality (i.e. you have relied on a rather unreliable internet source) then your argument may be less reliable too.
>
> • Try to avoid making an assertion if you do not have the evidence to back it up, as you will lose marks for this.
>
> • Evidence may be found in cases, statutory references, authoritative quotes or research findings.
>
> • You must reference the sources you have drawn upon in footnotes or endnotes (discussed in Chapter 6).

As indicated above, it is important to have evidence to back up the points that you are making. Indeed, each sentence that asserts an argument or sets out a principle should contain evidence and a footnote to the source of that evidence. Evidence may be in the form of cases, statutory references, quotes or ideas from academic work including theories, empirical research findings, and academic opinion on cases or legislation or on how law is working in practice. Newspaper debates or phone polls are evidence of what the public think about an issue, but they are not authoritative accounts of the law. You may use sources like this to supplement your legal sources if, for example, you are discussing how the law is perceived by the public, but do not use such sources as evidence of what the law is or how judges have decided cases. Your evidence is there to support your assertions and consequently it must prove your point.

Evidence should be used in the middle part of a paragraph, but you should not begin a sentence by referring to evidence, unless you go on in that sentence to explain the principle or idea to be discussed in the essay. You should tell the reader the point you are about to make before providing the evidence to back up that point. If you begin a sentence with a discussion of a case or a statute, then you are asking the reader to work out why it is important. It is similar to being in court as an advocate defending someone on trial for murder, standing up at the beginning of your submission to the jury and explaining that the police found a knife at the murder scene before proceeding to describe the knife in detail. If you then sat down, the jury would be left knowing a lot about a knife but without having any idea about how that helps your client's defence to the charge of murder. The jury have not been told the point of your exposition of the evidence and they could jump to any number of erroneous conclusions that do not help your argument in favour of your client. Instead, you need to explain the relevance of the knife to the jury in the hope that this will clear your client's name. Always explain your point.

2.7: STAGE 6: THE CONCLUSION

- Draw the issues and their relevance together.

- Take the points that you have made at the end of each paragraph to construct your conclusion.

- Do not introduce new ideas.

Once you have exhausted all the issues on your list and provided evidence to back them up, you need to complete your essay by writing your conclusion. Your conclusion is the answer to the question in summary form, taking into account everything you have said previously in your essay or problem question answer. If you have followed the structure set out above then you should be able to read through the first and last sentences of each paragraph and pull those together into a conclusion to the question. Try to avoid introducing new ideas into your conclusion, as these should have been dealt with in your essay already. Make sure that your conclusion accords with the rest of your essay, in other words, do not tack on a conclusion that you think the marker will agree with even though your essay is pointing in a totally different direction. There are rarely right and wrong answers in essays and it is better to write a conclusion that fits with your essay than to manufacture a conclusion that you think will be popular.

Next steps:

You may wish to find an example of an essay question, either from one of your course or module handbooks or from a past exam paper.

1 Read the question and dissect it. Do you understand exactly what the question is asking?

2 Read through your lecture and tutorial notes for the topic that forms the basis of the essay. What are the key issues that are pertinent to the question? List them.

3 Write a sentence after each of the key issues, summarising what it is.

4 Note down any evidence that you have in support or against each of those issues.

5 Consider how each of the key issues may help you to answer the question and write that underneath it.

6 Consider where you would go to find other evidence, were you to attempt to write a full answer to this question.

7 Then consider how confident you now feel at answering that question. Does this technique help you to focus on the task? How would you refine it for future essays?

You may now wish to try the test your knowledge question and compare your paragraphs against those at the end of the book.

Q TEST YOUR KNOWLEDGE OF ESSAY WRITING

• Have a go at writing an introduction, a middle paragraph or two middle paragraphs of your own, for the essay title used as an example above:

'The British Parliament was once supreme.' Discuss with reference to Britain's membership of the EU and its obligations in relation to the European Convention on Human Rights.

• Consider your paragraph structure. Does your paragraph begin with a sentence or sentences setting out the issue to be discussed, a middle section in which the discussion takes place, and a concluding sentence or sentences in which the issues within the paragraph are explained in the light of the question?

• You may wish to compare your paragraphs against those in the answer section towards the end of the book, and also to good, and not so good, examples on the companion website.

 * Visit the Companion Website for examples of good and bad practice.

SUMMARY

You may find the following essay writing stages assist you in writing essays. Do not begin these stages until you have completed those set out in Chapter 1.

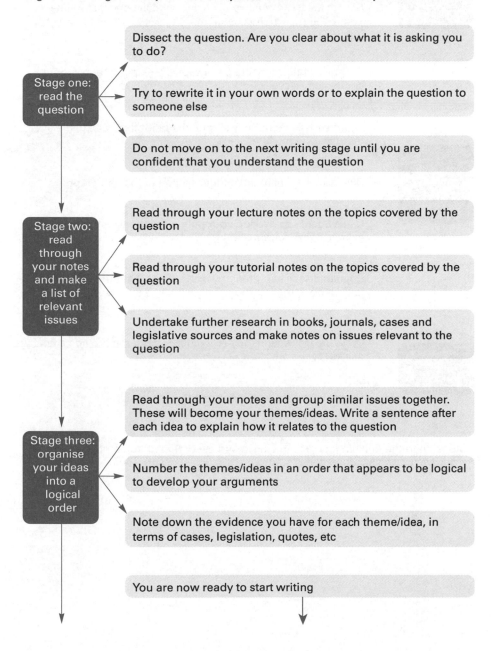

Stage one: read the question

Dissect the question. Are you clear about what it is asking you to do?

Try to rewrite it in your own words or to explain the question to someone else

Do not move on to the next writing stage until you are confident that you understand the question

Stage two: read through your notes and make a list of relevant issues

Read through your lecture notes on the topics covered by the question

Read through your tutorial notes on the topics covered by the question

Undertake further research in books, journals, cases and legislative sources and make notes on issues relevant to the question

Stage three: organise your ideas into a logical order

Read through your notes and group similar issues together. These will become your themes/ideas. Write a sentence after each idea to explain how it relates to the question

Number the themes/ideas in an order that appears to be logical to develop your arguments

Note down the evidence you have for each theme/idea, in terms of cases, legislation, quotes, etc

You are now ready to start writing

Stage four: write the introduction

Briefly explain the task that you are undertaking. You may wish to use the text of the question that you rewrote at an earlier stage

Set out the issues that you will deal with in your essay and how you will approach the question

Stage five: write the middle section of the essay

Organise your ideas into paragraphs. One paragraph should contain one issue

Begin each paragraph by stating the point that will be discussed within it

Discuss the point in the middle section of the paragraph

Use evidence to back up your points. Does each point have evidence that supports it?

Conclude each paragraph by explaining what the point means in relation to the question

Stage six: the conclusion

Draw the issues and their relevance together to provide a final answer to the question

Do not introduce new ideas into the conclusion

Move on to the finishing, polishing stages and check that all references to others' work are full and accurate (these stages are discussed in subsequent chapters).

3

ANSWERING PROBLEM QUESTIONS

Problem questions are vignettes—scenes set out for you to jump into and legal problems for you to diagnose. They are a form of role play and can be quite fun if you approach them in the correct way. They are similar to essay answers in some ways; however, they are designed to test different skills. Problem questions focus on a student's ability to diagnose the legal problem, to apply the law to the facts in the problem and to provide accurate advice on the likely chances of success if a case were to be taken further. They also test the ability to argue competing precedents, by arguing cases for and against the party to be advised. They consider how well a student can provide alternative courses of action to the client and to identify issues that may need further investigation before full advice can be given. This chapter will take a scenario that is public-law-based, and follow it through the process.

3.1: STAGE 1: READ THE SCENARIO CAREFULLY

- Read the scenario carefully.
- Reread it again.
- Make a list of facts and put them in chronological order.

We will work through the problem question set out in the introduction, to consider how best to approach writing an answer to a factual scenario. There are many ways to approach problem question answers; this is by no means the only way to diagnose the legal problem and to write an opinion on the legal options open to the party to be advised. However, if you are unsure about how to approach problem questions, this may be a good way to start the process.

The scenario is as follows:

Parliament has introduced a new licensing scheme to make sure that all individuals who want to work as art dealers must hold a licence. Parliament passes the Art Dealers Licensing Act 2008 and the Act states that the new Licensing Authority is responsible for administering the Art Dealers' licensing scheme. Section 2 states that *'The Licensing Authority may issue a licence to an individual to act as an art dealer if the individual has not been convicted of a serious criminal offence and if the individual has a recognised qualification in an art related subject.'* The Act further states that a degree in art or art history from a UK university will automatically be recognised for the purposes of the Act. Interim arrangements exist that require current art dealers to apply for a licence within six months of entry into force of the Act.

The following events occur:

Ruth works for an art dealer in London. Ruth is not sure whether she needs a licence as she currently does not sell art, she only values it. She has no criminal convictions and has a degree in art history from a UK university. She applies to the Licensing Authority for a licence just in case she needs to have one. Her application is refused. The Authority writes to tell her that she must stop her work immediately as she does not have the required qualification and she is not a fit and proper person to be an art dealer. In the letter the Authority tells her that the decision is final and cannot be challenged in any court whatsoever. Ruth telephones the Licensing Authority to see whether she really needs a licence and speaks to John, the decision-maker. He tells her that he considers that women do not make good art dealers or valuers. Ruth seeks legal advice from you.

The professional publication for art dealers runs an article in their journal about Ruth's situation. A reader of the publication, Phillip, hears of the problem and approaches Ruth to let her know that he would be willing to challenge the decision on her behalf.

Advise Ruth about her case and Phillip's suggestion to her about his role in bringing an action on her behalf.

Problem questions are relatively easy to approach, although the law that you need to apply may be complicated. First, read the scenario – obvious, yes, but it is tempting to jump in when you recognise something that you think you can write about. Next, read it again. You will not pick up on all the facts and the importance of the facts on the first reading. You may find it useful to write a list of events in chronological order, or, if you prefer, to draw a diagram showing who did what to whom, when and apparently why.

1   *Ruth works for an art dealer but is not currently an art dealer herself; she is an art valuer.*

2   *The Art Dealers' Licensing Scheme is introduced requiring all art dealers to have a licence in order to practise as art dealers.*

3   *Ruth applies to the Licensing Authority for a licence under the Art Dealers' Licensing Scheme.*

4   *Ruth applies on the basis that she has a degree in Art History from a recognised university and she has no criminal convictions, in keeping with the requirements of the Act. She appears to have met the requirements for a licence.*

5   *The Authority refuses Ruth's licence.*

6.   *Ruth is told that she must stop working in her current job as she does not have a licence. She is told that the decision is final.*

7   *Ruth telephones the Authority and the decision-maker tells her that he does not believe women make good art dealers or valuers.*

8   *Ruth wants to challenge the decision.*

9   *Phillip reads about Ruth's situation in the trade press and wants to challenge the decision on her behalf through the courts.*

10   *I have been asked to provide legal advice for Ruth.*

Hopefully by now you will have a good factual basis from which to work. Make sure that you identify for whom you are working, in other words, who is the client seeking advice. This will be important once you come to write up your opinion and it may also help you to bear this in mind when you are trying to work out the legal basis of the case. This is the factual analysis of the problem.

3.2: STAGE 2: FACTUAL ANALYSIS

> ● **Consider which of the facts are agreed.**
>
> ● **Consider which facts are disputed.**
>
> ● **Are there any facts that you need but have not been given?**

Consider which of the facts are agreed. In other words, which facts can you rely on as both sides share the same view of what happened? Which facts are disputed? In other words, where is there a difference of opinion about the facts? These will need to be argued in your answer. Are there any facts that you require but have not been given? You will need to say this in your answer to show that the solicitor will need to investigate these areas further, before you can provide a final opinion.

1   *Ruth works for an art dealer but is not currently an art dealer herself; she is an art valuer. – Not sure whether the Licensing Authority agrees that she is a valuer rather than a dealer.*

2   The Art Dealers' Licensing Scheme is introduced requiring all art deal-
    ers to have a licence in order to practise as art dealers. – Agreed.

3   Ruth applies to the local authority for a licence under the Art Dealers'
    Licensing Scheme. – Agreed.

4   Ruth applies on the basis that she has a degree in Art History from a
    recognised University and she has no criminal convictions, in keeping
    with the requirements of the Act. – Disagreement. She believes she meets
    the requirements; the Authority appears to believe she does not.

5   The Authority refuses Ruth's licence. – Agreed.

6   Ruth is told that she must stop working in her current job as she does not
    have a licence. She is told that the decision is final. – Agreed, factually,
    but Ruth believes that the decision is wrong and should be capable of
    challenge.

7   Ruth telephones the Licensing Authority and the decision-maker tells her
    that he does not believe women make good art dealers or valuers. – Not
    sure whether this is agreed with the Authority. The decision-maker may
    dispute this comment.

8   Ruth wants to challenge the decision. – Current position.

9   Phillip reads about Ruth's situation in the trade press and wants to
    challenge the decision on her behalf through the courts. – Current
    position.

10 I have been asked to provide legal advice to Ruth on her case and on the
    extent to which Phillip may bring a case on her behalf. – Current position.

3.3:   STAGE 3: LEGAL ANALYSIS

> • **Consider which area of law is the subject of the problem.**
>
> • **Look at the key concepts for that area of law and consider which may apply to the clients' situations.**
>
> • **List any tests that have to be considered for each of the concepts.**
>
> • **Plan your answer.**

The next step is to work out the legal areas that are relevant to the case. First pinpoint the subject area. You will probably have been given the problem question in a particular subject, for example, public law. Next try to work out the topic areas that are relevant to the problem. What do the facts suggest? Look back through your notes if you are not sure; the chances are that you have been lectured on the area already, or you will have been assigned reading to do in preparation for the problem. Once you have decided upon the topics that are relevant, reread your notes, then reread the problem. Finally extract the relevant issues from the notes you have from your lectures, tutorials and reading.

A broad outline of the legal area would look something like this:

Area of Law – public law case – judicial review according to Civil Procedure Rules Part 54.

Necessary requirements for a judicial review to be sought:

1. Decision-maker is a public body. Public functions test? See ex parte Datafin *(1987) and* ex parte Agha Khan *(1983).*

2. Clients must have standing – sufficient interest test s 31(3) Supreme Court Act 1981. Do Ruth and Phillip have standing under the sufficient interest test?

3. Judicial review must be brought within the time limit – no suggestion that out of time.

4. Relevance of the comment in the letter stating that she cannot challenge the decision in court? Is there an ouster clause in the Act? Does not appear so and in any event, see Anisminic. It looks as though there is no reason why the court would consider this issue non-justiciable.

5. Client's advocate must be able to argue at least one ground for judicial review – illegality, irrationality and procedural impropriety, including the rules of natural justice. Illegality and irrationality. Does not appear to be a procedural impropriety.

6. Client is seeking a remedy through judicial review.

7. Conclude by stating Ruth's chances of success and possible remedies and Phillip's chance of being permitted to bring the action on behalf of Ruth.

You may now begin to plan your answer in a similar way to the way that you would plan an essay. You should plan your answer by splitting up the issues in the same way as you would for an essay; in other words to assign one paragraph per issue and to plan each paragraph individually. Each paragraph should begin by explaining the issue to be discussed. The middle section of the paragraph should contain a development of the issue, with evidence to back up the points being made. The paragraph should conclude by explaining clearly what the legal issue means as regards the client's case, in this instance for Ruth and for Phillip.

3.4: STAGE 4: INTRODUCTION

- Explain the basic situation, briefly, and who you have been asked to advise.

- Set out the issues upon which you will give a legal opinion.

Problem question answers can be difficult to begin to write, because it is hard to know how to start off your answer. The simplest way to open your answer is to set out who you are advising and the nature of the case. Try to avoid reiterating all the facts in detail, as it will take too long and is unnecessary, as the client and the solicitor will already know the facts of the case. Some markers will prefer you not to explain the facts other than when they are relevant to the legal point that you are making. Do check this with your tutor, if you are unsure of current practice in your university. An example of an introduction for the problem question set out in the introduction would be as follows:

This sentence sets out the parties to be advised and the body against which an action will be sought

The sentence also identifies that the Licensing Authority must be a public body, which is a necessary condition for a judicial review action

In order to consider the merits of Ruth's case and to advise her (and Phillip) accordingly, it is important to establish whether the Licensing Body, the body that made the decision to refuse her a licence, is a public body susceptible to judicial review. In addition, it is necessary to consider whether Ruth and Phillip have standing to bring a judicial review case. The decision will be examined for elements of illegality, irrationality and procedural impropriety. Finally, the client will be advised on potential remedies.

This demonstrates the need for standing.

The third sentence sets out the substantive grounds to be considered

The final sentence states that the client will be advised on the strength of her case.

You should approach your problem question answer in a similar way to the structure set out above for essay answers. However, there are a few differences between essays and problem question answers. Problem answers deal with a set of facts and provide a legal assessment based on those facts. It is important that you know what you need to prove or disprove in order to provide an assessment of Ruth's chances of success, if the case were to go to court or to arbitration. If you are not able to put down the points that you need to establish then you are not yet clear on the law in the area. Return to your notes to work out what must be established in order to show that a contract has been established, or that the offence of theft has been committed or that Ruth is able to challenge a decision through judicial review.

From then on, until your conclusion, each issue should be discussed in turn in a separate paragraph. Look back at your introduction – what issues did you say you had to establish? Assign each issue one paragraph. Then plan the rest of your answer as follows:

3.5: ISSUE ONE ON YOUR LIST

- Write down the issue to be discussed.

- What do I need to establish to show that this issue has been proved or disproved?

- What evidence do I have to elaborate or to support these points in legal terms? Are there cases that are evidence for the general principles? Are there statutory extracts that are of relevance? Are there quotes or comments from academic texts that assist?

- Why is this issue relevant to Ruth and what does this mean in relation to Ruth's case?

All you then need to do is to write up that paragraph. The simplest way to do it is to follow the paragraph plan described in the previous chapter on essay writing. Your first sentence should set out the point you will deal with in your answer. This will be a description of issue one you highlighted in your planning stage:

It is important to consider whether Ruth is able to establish that the Licensing Authority that refused Ruth a licence is a public body, because public bodies may be judicially reviewed whereas most private bodies may not.

Or something along those lines.

Your next few sentences – the middle part of your paragraph – will take the reader through the principles that must be proved in order to establish whether or not, in this instance, the body is a public body. You should have evidence to back up every point you make. Evidence may be in the form of a case that establishes the test for what constitutes a public body – evidence could be a reference to a statute that sets out a test. Your evidence may even be in the form of academic opinion from a book or a journal article. You should be able to point to something that confirms what you are saying and it is important to back up your points; otherwise, as a barrister, you are saying to the solicitor, this is true because I say so (which generally is not going to be enough, and certainly could land you in very hot water if your advice is later found to be wrong!).

> *Ruth must establish that the body in question is a public body in order to mount a challenge to the decision through judicial review. The decision-making body is the Licensing Authority, which is exercising powers that have been conferred on it by statute and is administering a statutory licensing scheme. Its power is public in nature, similar to the power exercised by the Takeover and Mergers Panel in the case of* R v. City Panel on Takeovers and Mergers ex parte Datafin Ltd *[1987] QB 815 in which Lloyd LJ stated: 'if a body in question is exercising public law functions, or if the exercise of its functions has public law consequences, then that may be sufficient to bring the body within the reach of judicial review.*[1]

You may be able to provide more case law in support of this proposition. One case is a good start, but there are others that you could use to reinforce the point or to refine it. Even so, this is only two-thirds of the paragraph, even though many students move on to the next point at this stage and by doing so lose vital marks. You now need to apply the law to Ruth's situation. So far you have given general advice on the law in the area and this is not much use to Ruth who does not want to pay for a law lecture. The next stage, which will push you up to the next level of marks, is to say what the law means to Ruth. This is more straightforward than students think. All you need to do is to quickly reread what you have written, look again at your list or diagram of the facts that you drew up earlier on, and write a few sentences on how and why the law as discussed is relevant to Ruth. Does this mean she is in a strong legal position on this point, or a weaker position? Does this mean that she should be advised to take an action if the other side will not agree to her terms, or should she seek a different course of action? Your last sentence, thus, rounds off the point:

> *Consequently, the Licensing Authority's decision is susceptible to judicial review.*

---

1   Barnett, H. *Constitutional and Administrative Law* 7th edn (London: Routledge-Cavendish, 2008) p 690.

Once you have completed this stage in the paragraph you are ready to move on to a new paragraph to discuss the next issue on your list in the same terms. Once you have exhausted all the issues on the list, go back to the problem question. Is there anything in there that you have missed? Have you exhausted all the legal issues suggested by the facts? If not then continue with the paragraph system. Check your notes on the topic to be sure that there are no other issues that could be relevant to Ruth's case or to Phillip, who also wishes to challenge the decision. If so then you are ready to move on to the conclusion.

3.6: WHY USE EVIDENCE?

- **Do not make a statement unless you can back it up with evidence.**

- **Evidence could be (for example):**

- **Judicial opinion from a case;**

- **Sections from a statute;**

- **Views of a commentator: academic or practitioner, or other relevant spokesperson.**

3.6.1 HOW DO I USE EVIDENCE?

Evidence is just as it sounds – something to back up a point you are making. Evidence is never a point in itself and consequently you should not begin a paragraph by setting out your evidence. Instead, you need to explain what point you are going to make, then provide the evidence to show that what you say is true. You should try to avoid the following, in which a student has put the cart before the horse, the evidence before the point:

> In the case of *Anisminic v. Foreign Compensation Commission* [1969] 2 AC 147 the court held that errors of law may be reviewable in circumstances in which an ouster clause would ordinarily oust the jurisdiction of the court.

This could be simply rephrased to look something like this:

This sentence introduces the issue to be discussed

The second sentence provides relevant background to the issues

Ruth has to establish whether the comment made in the letter, which suggests that the Licensing Authority's decision could not be reviewed by a court, is backed up by an ouster clause in the relevant statute. An ouster clause is a provision in an Act, which ousts, or removes, the jurisdiction of the court in relation to any decision or action taken under the authority of the Act. There does not appear to be such a clause in the Act, but this will require further investigation. Further, there is judicial evidence to suggest that an ouster clause may not entirely remove the court's jurisdiction, even if one were present in the Act. The case of **Anisminic v. Foreign Compensation Commission** [1969] 2 AC 147 establishes that where there is an imputation of an error of law, the court will see past the ouster clause to consider whether an illegality has been committed by the decision-maker. This will override the ouster clause and permit the judicial review to be heard.

This relates the issue to the question and suggests the need for further investigation of the facts

This applies the law to the facts

This provides evidence in support of the legal principle

The final sentence provides a conclusion to the issue

Statutory references should be treated in the same way. They should be used as evidence of what the law is rather than to back up a point you are making. Quotes from academic texts are to be used similarly as are those from other sources.

3.7: CONCLUSION

- **Pull together all the legal evidence to provide an assessment of the strengths and weaknesses of the client's case.**

- **Provide the options open to the client.**

- **State any further investigation that may need to be undertaken prior to a final opinion being reached (if there are factual gaps or inconsistencies).**

The conclusion should summarise the strengths and weaknesses of the client's case and suggest the likely outcome if their case were to go to court. In addition, the conclusion may provide an assessment of the ways to settle the case using negotiation, mediation and arbitration. It may also set out any avenues that the solicitor will need to explore, before a final legal opinion may be given, for example any factual inconsistencies that may have a bearing on the case. The conclusion should not leave the solicitor or his or her client with unanswered legal questions.

Your conclusion should be one paragraph in which you provide your assessment of Ruth's chances of success if the case were to come to court. If you have followed the paragraph system it should be possible for you to read through the last few lines of each paragraph and, by pulling all of those together, show the strengths and weaknesses of Ruth's case. This determines what advice you would give on whether to go to court and if so what Ruth could expect to get. If your case is one for which the client may be entitled to damages, and you have not dealt with issues of quantum (level of damages) in your classes, then it is unlikely that your tutor will expect you to predict the amount of money the client would win. That said, you should be able to make a judgement on whether the client has a strong or a weak case and what they would be asking for if there are alternative remedies open to them. In a criminal case you would be giving an assessment of whether the client is likely to be found guilty, unless you have been asked to advise on other issues such as defences, for example.

Finally, you need to reread and polish your written work. Further guidance on this stage can be found in Chapter 7.

This chapter has shown that problem questions are relatively straightforward to write as long as you split the process up into small sections. Each paragraph is a self-contained unit, which sets out an issue, discusses the issue with evidence to back up the points that are made, and then concludes with an explanation of the relevance of the issue to the question. By building up the essay or problem question answer through single paragraphs, your answer should be well structured, clear and evidenced.

Next steps:

Now that you have read through the chapter you may want to review one of your own problem question answers.

1 First take a problem question that you have already attempted and carry out a factual analysis.

2 Carry out a legal analysis.

3 Read back through your problem question answer. Did you identify the pertinent facts and legal issues?

4 Looking at your answer, did you deal with each legal issue in a
separate paragraph?

5 Did you introduce each issue, discuss its relevance with the aid
of authoritative evidence and provide an assessment of how that legal
issue would be decided in your client's case?

6 Did you address all the legal issues that were relevant to your
client's case?

7 Did you provide a conclusion setting out the likely chances of
success were the client to go to court?

Now consider how you could improve your answer.

You may wish to visit the companion website for examples of good and
less good problem question paragraphs.

You may also wish to compare this way of approaching problem
question answers with the CLEO method. A good book to read on this is
S.I. Strong *How to Write Law Essays and Exams* 2nd edn (Oxford: OUP,
2006).

SUMMARY

The following stages may assist in approaching, structuring and writing answers to
problem questions.

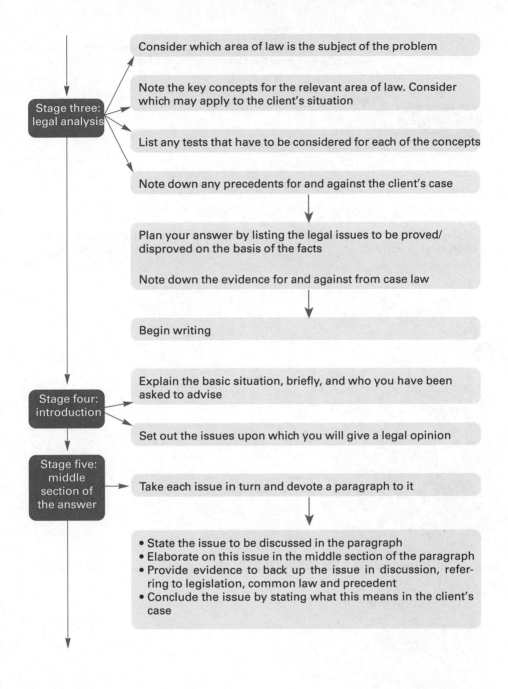

Stage three: legal analysis

Consider which area of law is the subject of the problem

Note the key concepts for the relevant area of law. Consider which may apply to the client's situation

List any tests that have to be considered for each of the concepts

Note down any precedents for and against the client's case

Plan your answer by listing the legal issues to be proved/disproved on the basis of the facts

Note down the evidence for and against from case law

Begin writing

Stage four: introduction

Explain the basic situation, briefly, and who you have been asked to advise

Set out the issues upon which you will give a legal opinion

Stage five: middle section of the answer

Take each issue in turn and devote a paragraph to it

• State the issue to be discussed in the paragraph
• Elaborate on this issue in the middle section of the paragraph
• Provide evidence to back up the issue in discussion, referring to legislation, common law and precedent
• Conclude the issue by stating what this means in the client's case

Stage six: conclusion

Pull together legal evidence to provide an assessment of the strengths and weaknesses of the client's case

Provide the options open to the client

State any further investigation required

Provide a final assessment on the client's case

Move on to the finishing, polishing stages and check that all references to others' work are full and accurate (these stages are discussed in subsequent chapters)

4 WRITING EXTENDED ESSAYS AND DISSERTATIONS

Extended essays and dissertations are very similar to standard essays in many respects; however, the depth and range of research is more extensive than for a 2,500-word piece of coursework. There are some differences, which relate to the way in which one constructs a question, and the way in which one sets about researching the dissertation. This chapter considers one way to approach dissertation writing, although there are many others.

4.1: STAGE 1: ESTABLISH THE TOPIC UPON WHICH YOU WISH TO WRITE

- Find a topic that is of interest to you.

- Read around the topic.

- Consider the sources available to you in the library.

- Discuss the topic with your supervisor.

- Finalise the topic upon which you wish to write.

The earlier that you can set your topic the better for your later research; much time can be wasted by swapping topics from one week to the next. However, it is important to know that the topic is of interest to you and also that there are sources available in the library to assist you in your research, particularly if you plan to undertake library-based research. You also need to make sure that your topic is one with which your supervisor is familiar and so you should choose your topic carefully and in conjunction with your supervisor.

4.2: STAGE 2: NARROW DOWN THE TOPIC

- The topic is likely to be far too wide to form the basis of a dissertation.

- You will need to narrow down the topic to a specific aspect of the topic.

- The more specific you can be, the easier it will be to research.

Students usually choose very wide topics upon which to write. This is, in part, a function of a lack of detailed knowledge in the area, a concern that a dissertation is an extended piece of writing and that the topic must be wide enough to allow a student to write 10,000 words. It is also in part, the fact that it is hard to be specific in the early stages of any research project. It is, perhaps, helpful to consider a dissertation as a research project – it is easier to undertake a project if you are clear on its parameters. The narrower the topic, the easier it is to research and also the easier it will be to show a depth of knowledge and analysis. Dissertations on broad topics tend to suffer from too much description; there is, after all, a lot to describe, and insufficient analysis and depth. The narrower the topic, the easier it is to demonstrate depth and thus to achieve higher marks.

4.3: STAGE 3: TURN THE TOPIC OR STATEMENT INTO A QUESTION

- It is easier to research a question than a topic or statement.

- Rephrase the statement as a question.

Dissertation modules often require students to come up with a research topic, a research question and then a dissertation that answers that research question. This is a departure from many other forms of legal writing, as for most assessments a lecturer will have set you a question rather than you having to develop your own. A dissertation is an enquiry to answer a question; it is not a discussion of a topic in general terms. It will be easier to focus your research and your writing on achieving your goal (a well-researched and presented extended piece of writing for which you will receive a high mark) – if you set a question early on in the process. It may be helpful for you to talk to your supervisor about which aspects of the topic you are interested in, and during that process try to come up with a broad question that encompasses your discussions, but which is sufficiently certain and discrete that it is capable of answer within your time period (usually two terms).

Once you have a research question, you should consider any sub-questions that need to be answered in order to present a final answer to the main question. What else do you need to establish before you can provide an answer to your main question? You may wish to list the sub-questions underneath your main question, by way of identification. If you think you have the answer to your question already in mind, then be honest about this and put this down on paper as a hypothesis – a proposition that you pose and which you then subject to research analysis in order to discover the extent to which you are right. A dissertation is not an exercise in proving your initial point; it is a process of enquiry to allow you to reach a considered decision on your question. However, if you do have an initial impression it is important to recognise this and to challenge it rather than to pretend you are open to all viewpoints when really you are trying to fit the evidence you find to the answer you want to provide in your writing.

You may begin the main part of your research once you have a title expressed in the form of a question. You may have had to do some background research prior to this, in order to know enough about the topic you have chosen and to be able to formulate the question. However, your main research phase will take place once you have fixed upon your question. There is more information in later chapters on the research process and on essay structure and referencing the work of others. Alternatively, refer to a text focused specifically on writing dissertations. One such book is provided in the Bibliography section towards the end of the book.

4.4: STAGE 4: START A 'RUNNING DOCUMENT' ON THE COMPUTER

- Once you have a title, start a 'running document' on the computer.

- Open a document, put the title on the first page, and then lay out the document as if it were a dissertation.

Include pages such as:

- Abstract/executive summary;

- Contents;

> - **Introduction;**
>
> - **Section 1, Section 2, Section 3, Conclusions, Bibliography.**
>
> **Use this document for notes, questions to yourself, lists of material to research, etc.**

Students, and academics, often put off writing. It is difficult to know how to start and one always feels underprepared for the task. Consequently, many begin writing just before a deadline, feel overwhelmed by the task and a little panicked. It is relatively easy to overcome some of these problems, although not the motivation to get on with the writing stage, by starting a running document on the computer. Consider setting up a Word document, or similar, split into sections. A dissertation will usually include a title page, an acknowledgments page, an abstract or executive summary page (in which the dissertation is summarised in 100–250 words for the marker), a contents page, an introduction, sections or chapters 1–3 or 4 (however many appear appropriate for the dissertation), conclusions, a bibliography and appendices. Students undertaking empirical work may include a research methods section or chapter in addition to an introduction, or may include this information in the introduction. Some may also set out a chapter as a literature review, in which academic literature on the subject of the dissertation is discussed, prior to undertaking original empirical research on the area. The literature in library-based research tends to be pervasive in the dissertation, rather than contained in a separate chapter. Discuss this with your supervisor if you are unsure about which is most appropriate for your enquiry. Format the titles, add in page numbers, make the document look like a finished document (but without any real content!) and use this as the place to write all your research notes, questions, comments and sources from now on.

4.5: STAGE 5: DISSECT THE QUESTION AND PLAN THE RESEARCH

> - **Analyse your own question.**
>
> - **List the issues that the question encompasses.**
>
> - **Make a list of general sources that could provide you with material for the dissertation.**

- Consider library-based sources; consider empirical sources such as interviews, questionnaire surveys; observation; analysis of official statistics, etc.

- Note down how these sources could assist in the dissertation.

- Plan your research.

- Write all of this within the 'running document'.

- Discuss this with your supervisor.

The next stages are similar to those for shorter essays, although your research will be much more extensive and may involve empirical research techniques (in which case talk to your supervisor about research methods, read up on them and keep a note of how you conduct your research and include this in your introduction or in a separate methods section). It is as well to plan how you intend to undertake the research phase of the dissertation in order to minimise the time that could be wasted in looking up material on areas that you will later discard. You may consider dissecting your own question to make a list of issues that need to be addressed in order to answer it, then transforming those issues into sub-questions. In a dissertation of around 10,000 words, it is probably only possible to deal with three to five issues effectively, although these too can be narrowed down into sub-sub-questions, if desirable. Review the main question and the sub-questions to consider whether these appear, if fully answered, to provide a full answer to the main question. Amend them as necessary. Add these into the running document and move on to the research planning stage.

4.6: STAGE 6: PLAN THE RESEARCH

- Analyse your own question and sub-questions. Do they still make sense to you? Do you need to revise your question, to narrow it or to broaden it?

- List the issues that the sub-questions encompass.

- Make a list of general sources that could provide you with material for the dissertation.

- Consider library-based sources; consider empirical sources such as interviews, questionnaire surveys, observation, analysis of official statistics, etc.

- **Note down how these sources could assist in the dissertation.**

- **Plan your research.**

- **Write all of this within the running document.**

- **Discuss this with your supervisor.**

This is an important stage, because it is probably only now that you can see whether your original question is too broad or too narrow, whether you will have access to the necessary research resources to answer it and indeed whether you even want to continue with the question drafted this way. You will continue to revise your question, and your research, in the light of your deepening knowledge of the area, but now would be a good time to assess, in realistic terms, whether this is the question that you want to take forward. You should do this in conjunction with your supervisor.

Once you have a list of sub-questions, note down what sources of data may provide answers to them, and where those sources can be located. You should use a range of sources for each sub-question, rather than restricting yourself to one source, as the more sources you use, the more likely you are to develop a balanced understanding of the issues and gain multiple forms of evidence with which to assert your arguments. This will provide breadth, depth and authority to your writing.

4.7: STAGE 7: BEGIN RESEARCHING THE INTRODUCTION

- **The introduction should explain the state of academic and legal knowledge on the main topic of your dissertation (unless the dissertation contains a separate literature review).**

- **Consult the library catalogue for sources relevant to your topic, within the library.**

- **Refer to journal articles on the topic.**

- **Conduct a search of electronic databases for relevant cases and legislation.**

- **Make notes for these in the running document under the introduction heading.**

- Note down the source of the notes, so that these can be turned into footnotes at a later stage.

The introduction in a dissertation is more extensive than an introduction in a traditional coursework essay. The introduction should set out how you have approached your dissertation research, including your research method, unless you have assigned a separate section to this method. It should explain the nature of the question and the sub-questions and how these aim to provide an answer to the main question. It should refer to academic literature written on the subject of your dissertation, as background, unless you have assigned a separate chapter as a literature review. This background provides the platform for your subsequent research on the sub-questions. The introduction should also set out the issues you will consider in the dissertation and explain the structure of the dissertation.

4.8: STAGE 8: CONDUCT RESEARCH ON THE NEXT SUB-QUESTION

- Follow the steps above for each sub-question.

- Refer to books on empirical research techniques if you are considering undertaking interviews, questionnaires or observational research.

- Make notes in the running document on material for this sub-question.

- Keep in touch with your supervisor.

The next step is to undertake research for each sub-question, as you would approach any other essay. Each sub-question is a mini-essay in itself, with an introduction, a middle section and a conclusion. Consider which sources will be relevant in answer to the question and where they are located. Make notes on each of the sources, preferably in the running document, with full references, including page references, for each source. Discuss your progress with your supervisor before moving on to the next section. Any material that you find while working on one section, which is relevant to another section, can be noted down within the relevant section for use at a later stage. Continue with note-taking until either you have exhausted the cases, legislation, academic works,

49

interviewees or participants, or until you wish to review the notes to date and begin to write them up into paragraphs.

4.9: STAGE 9: REVIEW YOUR NOTES FOR EACH SECTION/CHAPTER

- Reread the question.

- Read through the running document and consider whether the sub-questions appear to answer the main question.

- Read the notes you have made.

- Follow the essay writing steps in previous chapters to plan a mini-essay for each sub-question.

- Group issues together that appear similar and those that appear to be different.

- Construct paragraphs from your notes, using evidence to back up the points being made.

- Reread each section/chapter to review whether it answers the sub-question.

- Consider where there are gaps in your arguments.

- Conduct further research if necessary.

- Repeat the steps until you have fully answered the sub-question.

Some people prefer to complete the research phase for a section before starting to write the notes up into paragraphs. Others prefer to do both, alongside each other, in order to break up the monotony of note-taking. The writing phase for a dissertation is very similar to the writing phase for an essay, although more extensive. Similar rules apply, however, as set out in Chapter 2. Read through the notes and organise them into themes. Consider how each theme relates to the sub-question. Group any evidence that is relevant to the theme next to the theme and organise themes into a logical order. You are likely to change these around as the dissertation progresses and you will also write and rewrite paragraphs as you go along. However, do not let this prevent you from writing up your notes early on in the dissertation process, as much of the material you write now will be used in one form or another in the final draft. It is more satisfying to see the dissertation grow and to edit it down to the word limit later on in the process, rather than to try to construct a dissertation as the deadline approaches.

4.10: STAGE 10: READ THROUGH THE SUB-QUESTIONS AND WRITE THE CONCLUSION

- Read through the main question and the sub-questions.

- Read through each dissertation section/chapter.

- Write a conclusion on each section/chapter in the conclusions section.

- Write an overview of the concluding remarks made at the end of each of the paragraphs to provide a final conclusion to the dissertation.

Each section should contain a conclusion that pulls together a final answer to the sub-questions that you set for that section. The easiest way to approach the dissertation conclusion is to cut and paste each of those conclusions into the final conclusion section, read them through and edit them to form the new conclusion. Your final conclusion will also need to explain how each of the sub-questions (and conclusions to those sub-questions) fit together to provide a complete answer to the main question. Conclusions sometimes begin with a discussion of the main question – what the research project has sought to consider – and how the sub-questions seek to do that. You may then wish to write one or two paragraphs in respect of each sub-question, prior to finalising the conclusion with paragraphs providing the final analysis of the main question. Try to avoid introducing new ideas into the conclusion unless they are simply thoughts for the future, as new ideas may detract from your findings and lead the reader to wonder why you did not address them more fully in the main body of your work.

4.11: STAGE 11: FIRST DRAFT POLISHING – OVERVIEW

> - **Read through the main question and the sub-questions.**
>
> - **Read through each dissertation section/chapter.**
>
> - **Check that each section answers the sub-question fully, with evidence to back up any assertions.**
>
> - **Check that, when read together, the whole dissertation answers the main question, with evidence to back up any assertions.**
>
> - **If the question is not fully answered, could the question be amended so that the dissertation and the answer do fit?**
>
> - **If not, then rewrite the dissertation as required.**

The first review of your dissertation should focus on whether you have answered your main question and subsequent sub-questions. Take the main question and dissect it, as you would in an exam or for a piece of coursework. Does it really fit with what you have written in your dissertation? If it does not, if permitted under the module regulations, amend the title so that it does correspond with the task you have undertaken. You will be marked against your question and thus the dissertation must be a full answer to it.

Next, review the sub-questions. Do they appear, when taken together, to answer the main question? Undertake the same steps as discussed for the main question. Then read through each section or chapter to consider whether each one answers the sub-question fully. Each section is similar to a mini-essay and may be as long as a piece of coursework submitted at level 4. Each should have an introduction, a middle section and a conclusion, in the same way as any other essay. Each section should provide an answer to the sub-question set for that section.

The next step is to read through the introduction. Does the introduction set out how you have approached your dissertation research, including your research method? Does it set out the question and sub-questions? Does it refer to academic literature on the area you have researched? Does it set out the issues you have considered? Does it explain the structure of the dissertation? Make any changes to your draft, before turning your attention to the conclusion.

Finally, read through the conclusion. Does it pull together each of the conclusions from each of the dissertation sections? Does it provide a final conclusion to the main question, indicating how each of the sub-questions links to provide that answer? You may wish to read through each section conclusion again, before reading the final conclusion, to assist this process.

4.12: STAGE 12: SECOND DRAFT POLISHING – PARAGRAPH MAPPING

- Read through the dissertation paragraph by paragraph.

- Check that the paragraph begins by stating the issue to be discussed within it.

- Check that the paragraph contains a discussion of the issue.

- Check that the paragraph contains evidence to back up the discussion of the issue.

- Check that full citations have been included to others' words/ ideas and that those citations are included in the bibliography.

- Check that the paragraph is concluded with a sentence or sentences, explaining how the issue relates to the sub-question.

- Check that the paragraphs flow on from one another so that the arguments develop logically, and all similar issues are dealt with together.

- Make any changes.

Read through your draft again, if you can bear it. This time you are mapping each paragraph. Check that each paragraph is clear on the issue being discussed, the evidence in support of the assertions being made and the relevance of the issue to the sub-question. Check too that all sources are fully referenced in footnotes and relevant material is contained within the bibliography. Each sub-question should then be related to the main question in the conclusion, to provide a complete answer to the main question. It is also useful to note down on your draft the issue being discussed in each paragraph and then to skim through these notes to ensure there is no repetition. You should also check that similar issues are dealt with together. You may need to move paragraphs around in your draft, maybe even to another section in your dissertation, to cut down on repetition and to assist the development of your arguments. Make any changes and then move on to finishing and polishing your work.

4.13: STAGE 13: THIRD DRAFT POLISHING – SPELLING, GRAMMAR, PRESENTATION AND FORMATTING

> ● **Check your draft for spelling and grammar mistakes.**
>
> ● **Consider the formatting and presentation requirements set for the dissertation module and make sure your draft conforms to those requirements.**
>
> ● **Make any changes.**

This step is best undertaken after you have put your dissertation to one side for a few days. It is always easier to finish and polish a piece of work, once you have had some distance from your work (and also some sleep!). Read through your dissertation one final time, to proofread it. Run a spellcheck if you have not done so previously, so as to eliminate as many minor mistakes as possible. Check that sentences flow and that the dissertation is presented in a way that conforms to any formatting and presentation requirements, including line spacing, page numbering or layout. If you have used headings in your dissertation, check them to make sure that all headings of the same level look the same – are they all the same point size, in the same font, are they all bold, or italicised, or underlined? Although you are unlikely to lose marks for issues such as these, a well-presented dissertation gives an aura of authority. It is as well to project a professional image rather than an unprofessional one. You may wish to refer to Chapter 7 to consider writing style issues. Dissertations should be written in a formal style, unlike this book, which has adopted an informal style. Check, too, that footnotes and endnotes are all typed in a consistent style and that the bibliography is in alphabetical order, that it is complete, groups books with other books, journal articles with other journal articles, websites with other websites, and cases and legislation in separate sections. Make any changes before moving on to the final stage.

4.14: STAGE 14: FINAL CHECK OF ASSESSMENT AND GRADING CRITERIA

- Finally, read through the assessment and grading criteria for the module and check your draft against it.

- Make any changes.

Far more will be expected of a dissertation than a piece of coursework at levels 4 (first year) and 5 (second year). Make sure you have read the assessment and grading criteria before you begin your dissertation, but also read them through again at the end to ensure that your dissertation meets them. Reread any instructions given to you in relation to the dissertation – the number of copies that should be submitted, to whom, and so forth, prior to submitting your work. Then have the courage to hand it in, and congratulate yourself on having finished a large piece of writing.

Next steps:

1 Check your progress on the flow chart to see where you are in the dissertation process.

2 Review what you have done so far and consider which steps you have completed but, which on reflection, you may need to revisit.

3 Plan out your time between now and the deadline. Do you need to change anything about your work pattern in order to ensure successful completion?

4 Consider whether you need to see your supervisor to discuss progress. Have you got any written work ready to send to him or her in advance so that your meeting may be a productive one?

If you are in any doubt about research or referencing, you may wish to read the next two chapters.

SUMMARY

The following approach may assist in researching, structuring and writing a dissertation, although you should discuss your approach with your supervisor.

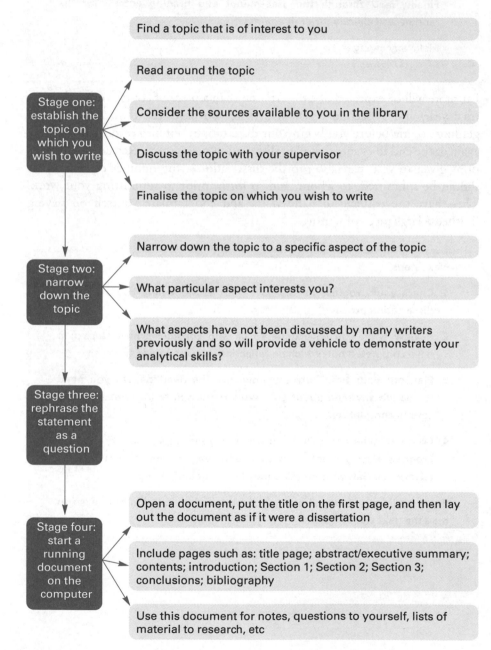

Find a topic that is of interest to you

Read around the topic

Stage one: establish the topic on which you wish to write

Consider the sources available to you in the library

Discuss the topic with your supervisor

Finalise the topic on which you wish to write

Narrow down the topic to a specific aspect of the topic

Stage two: narrow down the topic

What particular aspect interests you?

What aspects have not been discussed by many writers previously and so will provide a vehicle to demonstrate your analytical skills?

Stage three: rephrase the statement as a question

Open a document, put the title on the first page, and then lay out the document as if it were a dissertation

Stage four: start a running document on the computer

Include pages such as: title page; abstract/executive summary; contents; introduction; Section 1; Section 2; Section 3; conclusions; bibliography

Use this document for notes, questions to yourself, lists of material to research, etc

Dissect the main question; list issues relevant to the question

Stage five: consider the main question and list relevant issues

Group issues together to form themes. Turn these into sub-questions

Check whether the sub-questions appear to answer the question, if they are answered fully in the dissertation

Assign one sub-question per section or chapter in the running document

List the issues that the sub-questions encompass

Make a list of general sources that could provide you with material for the dissertation, including library-based and empirical sources. Note down how these sources could assist in the dissertation

Stage six: plan the research

Consider how these relate to each sub-question

Plan your research

Write all of this within the running document

Discuss this with your supervisor

The introduction/literature review should explain the state of academic and legal knowledge on the main topic of your dissertation

Stage seven: begin researching the introduction

Consult the library catalogue for sources relevant to your topic, within the library. Refer to journal articles on the topic. Conduct a search of electronic databases for relevant cases and legislation

Make notes for these in the running document under the 'introduction' heading. Note down the sources of your notes

Stage eight: conduct research on the sub-questions

Follow the steps above for each sub-question

Refer to books on empirical research techniques, if you are considering undertaking interviews, questionnaires or observation research

Make notes in the running document on material for this sub-question

Keep in touch with your supervisor

Stage nine: review your notes for each section and write up

Reread the sub-question

Read the notes you have made

Follow the essay writing steps in previous chapters to plan a mini essay for each section

Construct paragraphs from your notes, using evidence to back up the points being made

Reread each section to review whether it answers the sub-question

Consider where there are gaps in your arguments. Conduct further research if necessary

Repeat the steps until you have fully answered the sub-question, including an introduction, a middle section and a conclusion

Stage ten: read through the sub-questions then write the conclusion

Read through the main question and the sub-questions

Read through each dissertation section/chapter, paying special attention to each section conclusion

Explain the task set in the dissertation by way of introduction and how the sections sought to answer it

Summarise the conclusions reached in each section/chapter in the conclusions section

Pull these conclusions together in final answer to the main question

Stage eleven: first draft polishing – overview

Check that each section answers the sub-question fully, with evidence to back up any assertions

Check that, when read together, the whole dissertation answers the main question, with evidence to back up any assertions

Make changes as required

Stage twelve: second draft polishing – paragraph mapping

Read through the dissertation paragraph by paragraph

Check the structure of each paragraph, including the quality of the discussion of each issue, the evidence provided in support and the stated relevance of the issue to the topic

Check that full citations have been included for others' words/ideas and those citations are included in footnotes and in the bibliography

Check that the paragraphs flow from one another so that the arguments develop logically and all similar issues are dealt with together

Stage thirteen: third draft polishing

Consider the formatting and presentation requirements set for the dissertation module and make sure your draft conforms to those requirements

Consider the style of the dissertation. Are all the headings, paragraphs and footnotes consistent in style? Does the document look professional? Has it been written in a formal style?

Check the bibliography is complete, is grouped by source type and is ordered alphabetically by author's last name and then by year

Stage fourteen: final check of assessment and grading criteria and submission

Read through the assessment and grading criteria for the module and check your draft against it

Make any last minute changes

Hand it in!

5

HOW TO APPLY RESEARCH FINDINGS IN YOUR WRITING

You will need to research relevant law and related issues in order to answer your essay or problem question answer.[1] Research can be daunting, as there is a lot of information available and it is difficult to know how to find relevant information. You should be able to navigate your way through the research process successfully, if you break down the research process into manageable steps. The key stages in good library-based research for essays and problem questions are as follows:

5.1: KEY STAGES IN THE RESEARCH PROCESS

- Identify your question and dissect it.

- Carry out background research if necessary, to ensure that you understand the question. This should usually include reading through any lecture and tutorial notes on the topics covered by the question.

- Carry out textbook reading on the topic, making notes relevant to the question.

- Carry out research using the library catalogue to find any other texts relevant to the question. Make any additional notes that are relevant.

- Research cases and legislation that are relevant to the question and read important ones in full. Important cases will often be highlighted in your textbook. It is good practice to read these in full and in the original (rather than in the textbook).

---

1 Unless of course you are in an exam, in which case you will have done this before you enter the exam room, through revising the law and academic opinion on the law and legal concepts that you are likely to address in your exam answers.

- Research academic opinion on the topic by reading journal articles or academic texts and make notes on any issues raised that are relevant to the question.

- Read through all your notes and make a list of key issues from your notes, which are relevant to answering the question.

- Highlight any evidence you have in your notes in support of or against the key issues you will discuss in your essay.

- Make sure that you keep a record of all the sources you have used, including the page references of the material you have noted down.

- Plan your essay.

- Begin writing your essay.

You should spend a considerable period of time considering what the question is asking you to write about. This is the diagnostic phase of your role, and your ability to do well in the essay is dependent on correctly diagnosing the legal or socio-legal issues that you are being asked to discuss.

5.2: How to Start Your Research: What is Your Question?

- If you have been given a question, dissect this first and make sure that you are clear on what it is asking you to write about. This will make it easier to be focused during your research phase.

- If you have to set your own question for a dissertation, then define your research area in broad terms but make sure you have translated your research into a question rather than a statement to begin with.

As indicated earlier, understanding the question is the key to success. Either rewrite the question in different terms to be sure that you have understood it, or list the main issue that is the subject of the question and then any sub-issues that you should consider in the light of the main question. If you have not been given a question, then you need to define one for yourself. There is some guidance on this in the previous chapter.

5.3: USE YOUR EXISTING NOTES

> **Pull out your lecture notes and any other notes you have on the main subject of the question and read those through. This is your background research. Look back at the question.**
>
> **Write down any things from your notes that are relevant to the question, including any evidence you have that backs up the points you have noted down.**

You will hopefully now have a piece of paper that has the question written out on the top with a few lines underneath, which set out what the question is asking you to do. It is now time to turn to your lecture and tutorial notes to consider what material may be relevant to the question. This stage of your research will be made considerably easier, if you have a completed set of good quality notes. You will be taught for the most part of your degree programme through lectures and tutorials, sometimes referred to as seminars. You need to make the most of the limited contact time you have with staff, as this will reduce the amount of extra reading you need to do yourself in order to understand the basics of each topic. The lecture should take you through the key issues of a topic and, if you have made useful notes, these will form the basis of your background research.

5.3.1 NOTE-TAKING IN LECTURES AND TUTORIALS

Lecturers usually make a point, then expand upon the point and then provide evidence to back it up and further explanation to illustrate it. You do not need to write all of this down and the chances are that you will not be able to keep up, even if you do try to take down notes verbatim. It is better to listen to what the lecturer is saying, to write down the point that is being discussed, take a note of any evidence that is provided to back up the point (usually this will be a case, a piece of legislation or a theorist's viewpoint), rather than all the detail. This is not easy, and will take practice, but a transcript of the lecture will not make that much sense either. One example would be as follows:

> **Parliamentary supremacy lecture**
>
> **Meaning: Parliament has supreme legislative power.**
>
> **Main theorist Dicey, Jennings modified Dicey's theory, there are other views too.**

3 parts to theory:

A. Parliament can make, change, repeal any law without any restrictions at all.

B. The courts cannot question the legal validity of an Act of Parliament, nor can anyone else

C. To ensure that Parliament remains supreme, an earlier Parliament cannot bind a later one.

Evidence:

A. *Burmah Oil v. Lord Advocate* [1965] AC 75, War Damage Act 1965

See Jennings example in *The Law of the Constitution* smoking on the streets of Paris

B. Traditional interpretation: *British Railways Board v. Pickin* [1974] AC 765 Lord Reid quote at 782

But see alternative view: Lord Woolf in "Droit Public – English Style" [1995] Public Law 57, says there may even be limits on Parliament if it enacts legislation that is extreme and in total breach of human rights

C. Dicey's traditional view as above. But, redefinition theory – Jennings. Heuston. See Parliament Acts 1911 & 1949 for discussion on manner and form.

ECA 1972 – has Parliament bound future Parliaments through membership of EU?

. . .

This extract demonstrates the way in which many lectures operate. The lecturer will often begin by providing a brief overview of the topic so that you have a cursory understanding before you get into the detail. Often the main themes are spelt out at this stage, and it helps to note these down, preferably leaving yourself some space so that you can go back and fill in detail and evidence under each heading. If you cannot do that you may wish to number or notate each of the themes so that you can match up the detail and evidence with the theme at a later stage. It may help you to organise your notes and also save you time in the lecture and afterwards. The lecturer will often move on to take each of the themes in turn, and provide a more detailed explanation plus evidence to illustrate the points being made. This evidence is often extensive. There may be case and statutory citations and quotes from scholars and practitioners. You may not be able to get all of this down, but as long as you have the citations you can look them up later if you need to.

There are as many ways of taking notes as there are people, and your views on useful notes may change over time. Some people prefer to draw spider diagrams, for example, others to divide their paper into sections and allocate different sections to different types of information, that is, one column for headings, another for summaries of key points, another for related evidence, and so forth. With practice you will find a method that works for you.

Most lecturers will use visual aids or handouts to highlight the important issues, or will repeat the issues so that you can take them down. You will be able to supplement these notes with notes from textbook reading, so do not panic if you think that you have missed a point. You can check with the lecturer at the end of the lecture as well, if needs be. You will not be tested on whether you can remember everything that has been said in the lecture, but you will be tested on whether you understand the topic. Try not to miss lectures as someone else's notes will not be written in the same way as your own and will be no substitute for missing the lecture. Finally, do not ask your lecturer for his or her notes. You will not make yourself popular by admitting that you have missed the lecture and the chances are that the lecturer will not have a set of notes that make any sense to you anyway. Many of us talk from bullet points or the PowerPoint presentation we are using, rather than having a set of written notes in front of us.

5.3.2 PREPARATION FOR TUTORIALS

It is a long-standing sport among students, to see who can 'wing' the tutorial the most effectively. Of course, you may find that you can get through a tutorial or seminar unprepared, but it will be very little use to you in the long run, sadly. Tutorials and seminars are designed to test your knowledge and to make sure that you understand the tutorial topic. The questions that have been set are the vehicle for your tutor to examine your understanding and to deal with areas of misunderstanding or confusion. They are not designed for a tutor to give you an answer that you can learn for the exam. In fact if they were, then you would most likely do very badly indeed in the exams, unless you were asked exactly the same question again. As I hope this book illustrates, legal writing is about demonstrating your understanding, not your memory. Consequently good preparation for tutorials and seminars allows you to test your understanding and to practise your question dissection technique and essay and problem question planning skills, even if you do not write full answers to all the questions that have been set. You may be asked to hand in a written answer to the question, but even if this is not the practice in your law school, it is as well to write an answer to the question, even if only in note form, so that you get used to working out what questions are asking. Writing an essay or problem question plan, with evidence under each issue, will make it easier for you to participate in the class and also for your tutor to check whether you understand the topic fully. It will also develop your diagnostic technique.

5.3.3 COMPILING LECTURE AND TUTORIAL NOTES WITH TEXT-BOOK NOTES

You may wish to allow space in your lecture notes for any textbook notes that you make later on the topic. That way you will have all your notes in one place, which will make preparation easier for tutorials and also for assessments. Alternatively, you may wish to incorporate your lecture notes into your text-book notes; it is really up to you. There is guidance later on in this chapter on making notes from textbooks and other sources. The next step is to plan your research by working out what else you need to know or you need to consider further.

5.4: PLAN YOUR RESEARCH

> ● **Plan your research.**
>
> ● **What sub-questions do you have? Where will you find the answers? Do you have a range of sources including books, cases, legislation, academic opinion from journal articles?**

A good essay will contain information from a range of sources including book-based sources, cases and legislation, and from journal articles and other forms of academic writing. You may also include your own fieldwork if you have done a questionnaire survey or you have interviewed people as well. Most under-graduate research for coursework will be library-based, although extended essays and dissertations do lend themselves to empirical research as well as library-based research.

It is hard to know where to look for information in a large library at first, particularly if you are not used to doing research. Consider the range of sources available in the library and what these could contribute to your essay or problem question answer. Write a list of sources and what these could give to you. Next you need to consider the issues that should be researched for your essay.

5.5: LEGAL RESEARCH: HOW TO GO ABOUT IT

- Plan your research.

- What do you need to know? What is your question/are your questions?

- Do you have a general understanding of the topic yet?

- Do you understand any sub-question or sub-issues you have been asked to consider? If not, where will you look for information on these?

- What sources may assist you to answer the question?

- Plan which sources you will use to answer your sub-question.

- Keep a reference for each source, author, title, etc. and the page number at which you found the information.

Your lecture and textbook notes are a good place to start your research, but they should not be the only sources that you refer to. You also need to read the important cases in their full reported form (rather than in the textbook) and read any relevant legislation in its original form as well. Journal articles are a good source of information on current academic debates on the law and legal theory, and government reports may provide evidence of proposals for legal reform. You need to refer to a variety of sources to give depth to your understanding and to your written work.

5.6: WHERE TO LOOK FOR THE ANSWERS TO YOUR RESEARCH QUESTIONS

- **Actual law:** legislation and cases.

- **Legal opinion/arguments/theories:** books and journal articles.

- **Public opinion:** newspapers, polls.

- **Research findings by academics:** books and journal articles as well as research reports.

- **Government policy:** official reports and consultation documents.

A good piece of written work refers to a variety of sources in order to prove the points that are being made in each paragraph. Some points will be backed up with reference to case law or legislation, some with references to legal opinion in books or law journals. You will need to look through the library catalogue to find books that are relevant to your research. The library catalogue will also provide details of the journals that are held in the library. The key is to make sure that the books you use are current, not out of date, as law books tend to be updated frequently as the law changes.

Cases can be found in the law report bound volumes in the library or via one of the electronic facilities such as 'All England Direct', 'LEXIS', 'WEST-LAW', 'Lawtel'. Legislation can be found in *Halsbury's Statutes* and *Halsbury's Statutory Instruments* in print form or via *Halsbury's Laws Direct* in electronic form. Newer legislation is available online from the Office of Public Sector Information.[2] Some of the electronic facilities also have recent legislation contained within their databases. European legislation can be found in the *Official Journal L Series*, which is available in print form or in electronic form via the Europa website.[3] You may also make use of EUR-LEX, which is a free online European Law service.[4] There are also law libraries, which are becoming increasingly electronic; however, many sources are still available in book form as well. Your law school is likely to run training in how to use the law library and the electronic sources, and it is as well to get to grips with your research tools as soon as you can and preferably before you need to use them for your coursework. Ask at the library counter if you are in any doubt, as they will be able to point you in the right direction, refer you to research guides or tell you when training takes place. More detailed information on legal research is provided in books by other authors, references for some of which are given towards the end of the book.

Many students are very adept at using the internet as a research tool. This is a great skill and can prove extremely useful, as long as you locate authoritative sources. Search engines such as Google Scholar can help enormously with that, along with non-internet-based electronic databases as mentioned previously. Most law essays and the vast majority of problem question answers should rely heavily on the research evidence from authoritative sources such as judicial comment in cases, the text of legislation, academic opinion from textbooks and from journal articles. Official reports may provide evidence of government policy or other state agencies. That is not to say that you cannot provide evidence from other sources, but it is important to consider what these sources tell you. Newspaper reports are evidence of what

---

2 This can be found at http://www.opsi.gov.uk/.
3 This can be found at http://www.europa.eu.
4 This can be found at http://eur-lex.europa.eu/en/index.htm.

has come to the public's attention or of public opinion itself. They are not legal authority and they should not be used to support comments of what has happened in a particular case (unless they are from the Law Reports section), nor are they necessarily evidence of facts, as we know that newspapers can get things wrong. Internet pages are also potentially difficult to use as evidence for certain propositions you may be making. The content of an internet page is only as authoritative as the author. Anyone with some computer skills can post information on the internet. It does not mean that the information is accurate, so do not rely on anything unless you are sure that the source is a good one and is very likely to be accurate.

Equally, some internet sites are funded by groups with very particular political agendas. The content of their sites will reflect their political views. This does not mean that the information cannot be used in written work, but it is important to understand the authors' standpoint and to explain that the material may be partial. It may only put forward evidence in favour of their views, while leaving out evidence that is equally valid but against their views. The standpoint of any author tells the reader about how s/he will have used evidence in the document. Your arguments will have added weight, if you are able to explain the author's standpoint and subject the author's arguments to analysis yourself.

You will make use of primary and secondary sources in your research. Primary sources are extremely important and should form a major part of your research. These are sources that give you the most authoritative evidence. A primary source is 'the thing' itself, and not someone's interpretation of 'the thing'. Secondary sources (there are tertiary, etc., too) are sources through which others give their opinion or their interpretation of something. The boxes that follow provide an illustration of primary and secondary sources.

Primary sources of law: Legislation

The legislation in *Halsbury's Statutes* or the official government site for legislation www.opsi.gov.uk, or in one of the scholarly legal databases (Westlaw, LexisNexis, Lawtel)

Things to check:

- Is the legislation in force?

- Is the copy of the legislation that you have, up to date?

Primary sources of law: Cases

The official application of the law – cases reported in the Law Reports (copies of which may be found in scholarly legal databases Westlaw, LexisNexis, Lawtel)

Things to check:

- Does the case squarely relate to this issue that you are considering?

Primary sources of law: Legislation

- Is the legislation applicable to this jurisdiction (Scotland only, Wales only, Northern Ireland only, England only, a combination of all four)?

- Is there associated primary or secondary legislation that you need to read too?

- Is the legislation in the process of reform?

Primary sources of law: Cases

- What is its precedent value –the seniority of the court? Binding or persuasive?

- Is the precedent still subsisting?

- Are there other cases that affirm this legal interpretation?

- Are there cases that contradict this legal interpretation? If so, how? What difference would it make?

- If the case is applied to the facts in the problem in front of you, what would be the result and why?

You may also make use of secondary sources. Secondary sources in this context would include:

Secondary sources for the law

- **Commentary on the legislation** – *Halsbury's Laws* – in the reference section of the library.

- **Commentary on the law** – General or specific comment or analysis by academics and practitioners, which are published in academic journal articles, academic books, textbooks. Many journal articles can be found on the scholarly legal databases. Books etc., via the library catalogue.

- **Less authoritative commentary** – wider public interpretation of the law (may be authoritative, may be totally inaccurate). This commentary may be found in many fora.

You will be asked to undertake research on areas other than the strict law, or government policy. For each of these you need to consider what question you are asking, in order to identify what would be a primary source of information on that, and what would be a comment/interpretation and thus a secondary source. You will need to use multiple sources of research evidence in your essay or problem question answer. Just as in natural science (when a scientist performs an experiment at least three times to judge the validity of the initial finding), a good researcher will seek multiple sources of evidence before reaching a conclusion. One source is not enough to make a proper assessment of a situation; it will also be insufficient to demonstrate the breadth and depth of your research skills and your scholarly credentials. One case is not evidence of the law, nor is one textbook or one journal article evidence of academic opinion as it may be only evidence of one person's academic opinion. Do not finish your research just because you have found one source to evidence each point. You must conduct broad and deep research, before you finalise your own conclusions.

Another issue, which is particularly relevant in relation to sources found on the internet is how authoritative is the source that you are considering? Your point is only ever as good as the evidence that you provide in support of it. But how do you know if your evidence is any good? How do you judge the authority of the source that you are reading? You should ask yourself the following questions:

> **How to judge the authority of a source**
>
> ● **Who is commenting?**
>
> ● **What is their standing and expertise?**
>
> ● **Are they commenting on something within their expertise?**
>
> ● **Have others reviewed this person's view and endorsed it (in other words has the work been reviewed by an editor or by other academic/ practitioner reviewers)?**

Books and journal articles are much easier to rely upon, as they have been through some form of review process to ensure at least basic standards of accuracy are met. However, some material on the internet will not have been reviewed or edited. Indeed, some of it will be misleading or possibly incorrect. Many lecturers will consider open-access sources that can be freely edited by anyone, such as Wikipedia, as unreliable in view of this fact. Some entries will be written to a very high standard and others will not. On that basis it is probably safer not to rely on them, but to find a more readily authoritative source that you can use instead.

Finally, textbooks are a good source of information, but a piece of coursework should contain a range of sources, not just references to the set textbook. Revision aids are just that – revision aids. They are good sources of basic information but they are not sufficiently authoritative to be a major source of evidence for a piece of coursework. Try to broaden out your research to include a range of sources, authors from a range of standpoints, and to use authoritative sources.

Before we move on to the next issue, it may perhaps help were we to consider the research steps required to locate authoritative evidence for the essay question set out in Chapter 2. After dissecting the question and reading through all lecture and tutorial notes, a relatively standard approach to research would be as follows:

1 Library catalogue search to find further textbooks (other than the one(s) used for the tutorial topic related to the question). You may also locate more scholarly texts (non textbooks) written for an academic audience. These may be more difficult to understand but would provide good research evidence. These should be authoritative secondary sources.

2 A LEXIS and/or WESTLAW search for relevant cases, legislation, journal articles. This type of research will give you primary (cases and legislation) and secondary authoritative sources (journal articles).

3 A visit to the EU's website (www. Europa.eu) and the Council of Europe's website (www.coe.int) may provide some background to help you with your study, or you may wish to use the search facilities to find primary and secondary sources there too. These would also be authoritative.

4 A Google Scholar search may provide you with more journal articles, which assist you in writing your essay and providing evidence in support of your points. Most of the sources here will be secondary and authoritative.

5 If you do wish to do a traditional internet search, using Google or one of the other search engines, be aware that many of the sources will lack authority and it may be difficult to authenticate the contents of many of the sites.

Now that we have considered, in brief, how to undertake research, we shall turn to how to make use of research findings in written work.

5.7: WHAT NEXT?

- Make notes on the issues that you need to answer in the question from your sources.

- Do not make general notes on the topic as you will not use that information and your effort will be wasted.

- Note down the full citations as you will need to reference your work.

Once you have found sources of information that are relevant to your essay or problem question, you need to begin making notes on the sources. Photo-copying the material and highlighting passages in the text is not the same as making notes! You may find it useful to highlight sections, but then you need to translate those sections into something that you can use. Your notes need to state the point that the highlighted section proves or disproves, as a quote is only evidence for the point you are making; it is not a point in itself. Return to your question frequently to refresh your memory about the task you have been set, and make notes according to the question rather than according to the topic. Ask yourself whether you will use the material you are writing down, and if not then do not take the time and energy to make notes on it.

5.8: HOW DO I MAKE NOTES FROM MY READING?

- Do not make notes straight away, read a paragraph or short section through first.

- Identify what point each paragraph is making.

- Make a note of that point; do not write out the paragraph again in your own words! Make a note of any evidence the author uses to back up the point.

- Write down the page reference so that you can find it again if you need to and so that you can footnote your source in your essay or problem question answer.

- Repeat for each short section.

- Always keep a full reference to your source, including an accurate page reference.

It is often more effective to read a section in the book or case report and then write notes about the main points at the end of the section rather than writing at the same time as reading (and therefore simply copying out the whole book in your own words). It is more important that you know the general principles and have evidence to support those in your written answer, than that you have hundreds of facts to write about. Your notes should be angled towards general principles rather than containing large quantities of factual information, which is really evidence for the points being made by the author of that work rather than the points that you need to make in your essay or problem question answer. You do need to note down evidence to support the points being made by the author, but this is evidence and should not be confused with the point being made.

5.9: HOW MUCH DETAIL AND WHAT NEXT?

> - You do not need all the detail in the textbooks, and you will remember more than you think if you read it through and concentrate on what you are reading, rather than reading and writing at the same time.
>
> - It is more important that you understand an area of law, than can remember the detail but not understand the important points.
>
> - Read through your notes and organise them into themes or display them as diagrams if that helps you.

Cases are an important part of the study of law. They are evidence of what the law is. You do need to read cases and to know their ratio and any important points made by judges in their *obiter dicta*. It will be sufficient for most cases to have a basic understanding of the facts as well as an understanding of the legal reasons for the decision – why in legal terms X won the case and Y lost the case. This is the information that you will need in problem question answers. In essay answers you are more likely to need to know the general principles of law that were established as a result of the case.

Academic articles give you a much deeper understanding of a subject area, although you may find them difficult to read to begin with. They are particularly useful if you are writing essays rather than problem questions. You should aim to read one article on each tutorial subject area to deepen your knowledge, but only after you have completed your textbook and case reading. The same rules apply for reading articles as for reading textbooks: read to understand and not simply to remember. You will not need detailed notes on articles, but you will need to understand the main points that the writer was making.

5.10:   ORGANISE YOUR IDEAS

- **Read through all your notes and collate your information into themes or issues.**

- **Return to the question and review your information.**

- **Organise the themes you have ready to assist in planning your essay.**

- **Include the evidence that relates to these issues.**

Collate your information by reading through all your notes again and pulling together the themes you identify. Write down each one with any discussion you have found, as well as the sources you have referred to. Return to the question and consider the themes you have from your notes. What do these themes tell you as regards the question? What issues are relevant to the question and why? What evidence do you have for your thoughts about relevant issues? Evidence may be in the form of judicial opinion from a case, sections from a statute or other piece of legislation or the views of a commentator – academic or practitioner – or other relevant spokesperson. Organise the evidence under each theme ready to begin your writing.

5.11:   MAKE SURE YOU REFERENCE THE
WORK OF OTHERS

What is it?

It is attributing the work that belongs to someone else to which you refer in your essays and presentations.

Why?

It should be possible from your references for someone else to go to look up the other's work and read it in its original source.

You need to take down the reference of any source you will use as part of your writing so that you are able to provide a reference to it in your written work. A full reference will include the page number from the page you have taken the information, so write this down at the time you are doing the research next to any notes you are making, otherwise you will have to go back to the library to try to find it before you can hand your work in.

Making Use of Evidence in Your Writing

- When you use evidence you demonstrate your skill (or lack of skill) as a scholar.

- You should provide as much evidence as you reasonably can, to back up the points that you are making.

- However, try to describe the evidence in as little detail as you can, in order to make your point effectively.

- Always provide a full citation to your evidence.

- Always introduce the point that you want to make first, before providing the evidence in support of the point.

- Finally, sum up your point at the end of your paragraph, so that the reader understands the conclusion that you have reached, in the light of your evidence.

It is difficult to underestimate how important is your use of evidence in an assessment. A 2.2 answer can jump to a 1st class answer, if sufficient evidence is used to add depth to arguments and authority to the points being made. Thus, good research and note-taking are really important phases in excellent work. There are some examples on the companion website that illustrate this point. But, it is also important to make sure that when you use evidence, you do so either in the form of quotes or as a paraphrased section. This means that you must either properly quote from the source to which you refer, and provide a full reference to demonstrate its origin, or you must summarise the section that you are reading in your own words and then provide a full reference to the source including the source's name. The next chapter will take you through this in more detail.

Next steps:

You may wish to review your approach to research. How do you usually conduct research for essays and research for problem question answers? Consider the following:

- How systematic is your approach to research?

- How knowledgeable are you about the research resources that your university holds? Have you looked at any of the library research guides?

- How much use do you make of primary sources of law?

- How much use do you make of secondary, authoritative, sources?

- Do you check the authority of secondary sources from the internet before you use them?

Next, think about how you take notes from the sources that you have located. How much do you focus your notes on the question posed? Or do you tend to take general notes, may of which you do not use in your assessments?

To what extent are you clear on when you are quoting someone's words, or summarising them entirely in your own words (paraphrasing)? Do you always note down full and accurate citations? You may wish to read the next chapter if you are in doubt about how to do this properly.

You may also wish to undertake the library familiarity task to prepare yourself for your next assessment.

There are more resources on the companion website to help you.

5.12: PREPARATION PRIOR TO YOUR RESEARCH: LIBRARY FAMILIARITY

You may find it useful to familiarise yourself with your law library and research sources before you begin your research. Pick up copies of your library's guidance leaflets or work your way through the following task to familiarise yourself with the sources of information available to you and where they are located.

5.12.1 TEXTBOOKS

What subjects are you studying this year? Where would you find textbooks for those subjects in the library? Where would you find study guides to help you with your skills development?

5.12.2 LAW REPORTS

What law reports does your library hold? Which ones are available in bound volumes on the shelves? Which are available in electronic format? Which electronic databases are available to you and how do you use them to search for cases?

5.12.3 LEGISLATION

Where can you find copies of *Halsbury's Statutes, Halsbury's Statutory Instruments* and the *Official Journal?* Do you have access to these sources in electronic form in your university and if so what do you need to do to be able to access these sources?

5.12.4 JOURNALS

What journals does your library subscribe to? Where are they located? Which ones are available in electronic form? How do you search them for relevant articles?

5.12.5 OTHER LIBRARY SOURCES AND SERVICES

What other sources of information are available in your library? How do you access them? Is training provided for you in the use of the databases and search facilities and how do you go about getting the training you need?

SUMMARY

You may find that you can save time on research and find relevant material, by following these key stages in the research process.

> Identify the task set in the question, by dissecting it word for word

> Carry out background research if necessary, to ensure that you understand the question. This should usually include reading through any lecture and tutorial notes on the topics covered by the question

Carry out textbook reading on the topic, making notes relevant to the question

↓

Carry out research using the library catalogue to find any other texts relevant to the question. Make any additional notes that are relevant

↓

Research cases and legislation that are relevant to the question and read important ones in full

↓

Research academic opinion on the topic by reading journal articles or academic texts and make notes on any issues raised that are relevant to the question

↓

Read through all the notes that you have made and make a list of key issues from your notes that are relevant to answering the question

↓

Highlight any evidence you have in your notes in support of or against the key issues you will discuss in your essay

↓

Make sure that you keep a record of all the sources you have used including the page references of the material you have noted down

↓

Turn this information into a plan, as discussed in Chapters 2, 3 and 4

↓

Begin writing your essay

6 CORRECT REFERENCING

Excellent academic written work is littered with research evidence, as discussed in the previous chapter. Referencing and citing others' work (along with primary legal sources such as legislation and cases) is one way of demonstrating your scholarly research skills. It demonstrates the wealth of material that you have found during your research phase. It provides authority and weight to your arguments. In short, it is a very good thing. Some students think it is better to pretend that they have come up with an idea, than to show that they have got the idea from something they have read. In fact, the opposite is true. Excellent work proudly shows off the sources that have been used in the writing process. In contrast, poor work provides few sources, but instead claims originality. Few academics will come up with a new original theory in their lifetime, and so we hardly expect undergraduates to do so. Even if you do manage to come up with a new theory, we shall still expect it to be built on solid (research) foundations. In this chapter we shall address the nuts and bolts of how to reference or cite others' work. But first we shall deal with a related issue: quoting and paraphrasing.

Why have I included quoting and paraphrasing in this chapter? It could have been placed in the previous one, but equally it fits well with referencing issues. There are two main options when you read something that is relevant to your essay or problem question and you wish to refer to it in your own work. You may either quote the relevant passage, or you may paraphrase it. The difference is as follows:

> **Quoting** – Copying word for word what someone else has written and enclosing the passage in quotation marks, providing a reference to the original source.
>
> **Paraphrasing** – Reading what someone else has written. Putting the source to one side (so that you do not inadvertently copy it) and then summarising the essence of what they have said entirely in your own words. Then providing a reference to the original source.

When should you quote, and when should you paraphrase? Quotations may be good evidence to support a proposition you are making. As stated previously in this book, quotations are no substitute for making your point, but they may be evidence to back up a point that you are making. If you are referring to the words of others, you must indicate that the words belong to someone else by putting them in quotation marks in your text and providing a reference to where you found them, usually in a footnote or an endnote.

A quote would be displayed as follows:

> 'Political and legal sovereignty – from the standpoint of sovereignty within the state as opposed to sovereignty as understood in international law – may be analysed as meaning either the supreme legal authority within a state or the supreme political authority within a state.(2).'[1]

Quotes of more than three or four lines long are usually indented and put on a separate line from the rest of the paragraph, as above. Shorter quotes would normally be set in the paragraph as normal. All quotes would normally be displayed with quotation marks. The usual form is to use '. . .' as quotation marks and then ". . ." inside the first set of quotation marks, but few lecturers will be too worried about the type of quotation marks you use as long as you stick to a consistent style. Check with your lecturer to find out whether there is a style guide if you are unsure, particularly in respect of longer pieces of course-work such as dissertations.

However, it is not often necessary to use quotations, because the point being made by your source may be better and more concisely made by you. Paraphrasing is really the means by which you summarise what someone else has said, in clear and concise terms. However, this is also something that many students struggle with, because they say the original author said it better in their own words. This may be true to an extent, but it often masks the real problem, which is that the student does not fully understand the phrase that they wish to use. It is hard to summarise something that one does not properly understand. You may need to give some thought to what the writer is trying to say (they may not have expressed themselves very clearly) and you may need to look up some of the words. But, one of the benefits of paraphrasing someone else's words is that you get more credit for having taken the time to get to grips with the idea (whereas you only get credit for finding and using a quote). You can also explain the idea in concise terms and so save some words on an assessment with a tight word limit. But, paraphrasing does need to be done properly, meaning that you need to use your own words, rather than changing a few words in the original

---

1 See Rees, W. J. 'The theory of sovereignty restated' in Laslett, 1975, Chapter IV as cited in Barnett, H. *Constitutional and Administrative Law* 7th edn (London: Routledge-Cavendish, 2008) p 134.

passage. Failure to do so may lead to a charge of poor scholarship or worse still plagiarism. As a result, some students avoid paraphrasing like the plague. But, paraphrasing is a skill like any other, and it is relatively easy to learn. Here are some examples of well-paraphrased and poorly paraphrased passages:

> **Original passage taken from H. Barnett *Constitutional and Administrative Law* 7th edn (London: Routledge-Cavendish, 2009) p 146 para 1**
>
> **Parliament may also legislate with retrospective effect, as with the War Damage Act 1965. The War Damage Act effectively overruled the decision of the House of Lords in *Burmah Oil Company v. Lord Advocate* (1965). In 1942, British troops had destroyed oil installations in Rangoon, with the intention of preventing them from falling into the hands of the Japanese. The British government made an *ex gratia* payment of some £4 million to the company. Burmah Oil sued the government for some £31 million in compensation. The House of Lords held that compensation was payable by the Crown for the destruction of property caused by the exercise of the prerogative power in relation to war. The government immediately introduced into parliament the War Damage Bill to nullify the effect of the decision.**

An example of good paraphrasing would look like this:

> **Parliamentary supremacy permits parliament to legislate in any terms. It may even pass legislation that has retrospective effect, even if that means, as is the case of *Burmah Oil Company v. Lord Advocate* (1965), this effectively renders a court decision ineffective.[2]**

This passage summarises the main arguments accurately and succinctly. It does so in the author's own words rather than by using most of the same words from Barnett's original passage. It leaves out the description that is not needed to make the point, but it does provide the legal evidence in support of the point. There is also a full and accurate citation to demonstrate that this is Barnett's work paraphrased, rather than the student's own ideas. However, an example of poor paraphrasing would look something like this:

---

2 Barnett, H. *Constitutional and Administrative Law* 7th edn (London Routledge-Cavendish, 2009) p 146.

> Parliament may also legislate retrospectively, as seen with the War Damage Act 1965. The War Damage Act overruled the decision of the House of Lords in *Burmah Oil Company v. Lord Advocate* (1965). In 1942 British troops destroyed oil installations in Rangoon, because they wanted to prevent them from failing into the hands of the Japanese. The British government made a payment of around £4 million to Burmah Oil. Burmah Oil sued the government for £31 million. The House of Lords held that the Crown had to pay compensation for the destruction of property caused by the use of the prerogative power in relation to war. The government immediately introduced the War Damage Bill to nullify the decision.[3] This is evidence of parliamentary supremacy in operation.

This passage is virtually copied word for word from Barnett's original text. However, as it is not included in quotation marks, the student is suggesting that the words are entirely her own. This passage either needed to be a proper summary of Barnett's ideas, in the student's own words, or an accurate quotation of them instead. This would likely be marked down for poor scholarship. The student has at least provided a full reference to Barnett's work, so there does not appear to be an attempt to deceive the reader into believing that the ideas are the student's own. But the student has given the impression that she has written this passage herself, when it is clear to us that she has really only edited Barnett's original text rather than summarising it herself.

Worse still, is the next example, which is an out and out example of plagiarism. The student has copied sections of Barnett's work without enclosing them in quotation marks, or providing a reference to the source of the words or ideas.

> Parliament may also legislate with retrospective effect as with the War Damage Act 1965. The War Damage Act overruled the decision of the House of Lords in *Burmah Oil Company v. Lord Advocate* (1965). In 1942 British troops had destroyed oil installations in Rangoon, with the intention of preventing them from failing into the hands of the Japanese. The British government made an ex gratia payment of £4 million to the company. Burmah Oil sued the government for £31 million in compensation. The House of Lords held that compensation was payable by the Crown for the destruction of property caused by the exercise of the prerogative

---

3 Barnett, H. *Constitutional and Administrative Law* 7th edn (London Routledge-Cavendish, 2009) p 146.

> **power in relation to war. The government immediately introduced into parliament the War Damage Bill to nullify the effect of the decision. This is evidence of parliamentary supremacy in operation.**

This would be taken very seriously indeed. And in addition to the issue of plagiarism, the student has thrown away the opportunity to show off her research skills and the evidence that she has to support what she could have said had she taken the trouble to do so. So there are two issues here: first, has the student properly quoted or paraphrased the evidence that she is relying upon? And second, has she provided a full and accurate reference to the sources of those words or ideas (the evidence)? We have addressed the first of these, so we shall turn our attention to the second.

Many students get very concerned about being found guilty of an assessment offence such as plagiarism, as academics are increasingly preoccupied with the problem of plagiarism and are stressing the importance of correct referencing in legal writing. Referencing can be a confusing business to begin with, but there are some simple rules that may help you with your writing and referencing, to make sure you steer clear of trouble. Put simply, referencing is giving credit to the author who had the idea or wrote the words that you are making use of in your essay or problem question answer. There are two broad schools, or ways of referencing: one known as Harvard (also sometimes called in-text referencing) and the other Oxford (also sometimes known as numeric). Harvard style referencing provides a brief reference to the author and his or her work at the end of the relevant sentence, followed by full citations at the end of the written work in endnotes or a bibliography. Oxford referencing makes use of footnotes instead. You can see examples of both on the companion website. The OSCOLA guide (The Oxford Standard for Citation of Legal Authorities) is a particularly helpful and comprehensive guide on how to cite UK, EU and international legal sources.[4] The remainder of this chapter will focus on domestic legal sources, and so you may wish to consult the OSCOLA guide for non-UK ones. It is currently being updated and a new version may be published shortly. It is well worth taking a look at it.

---

4 You may find it at: http://denning.law.ox.ac.uk/published/oscola_2006.pdf.

6.1: WHAT IS REFERENCING?

> It is attributing the work that belongs to someone else and which you are using in your essays and presentations.
>
> It should be possible for someone else to look up the other person's work and read it in its original source after looking at your references.
>
> If you do not reference properly you may either be found to have undertaken poor scholarship which will lose you considerable marks, or you may be found guilty of plagiarism which has serious penalties attached.

Many of the points that you make in your writing will be points made previously by other people. That is the nature of undergraduate study and it shows that you have carried out research, for which you will receive credit. However, when you use someone else's idea or you use their words, you must also give that person credit by stating that the idea or words were theirs first. You may be found guilty of poor scholarship if you do not cite all your sources, for which you will lose marks, or you may be found guilty of plagiarism if it is considered that you set out to pretend that the idea or words were yours. Plagiarism can lead to very serious penalties, including expulsion from your course. A law school may be under a duty to report your offence to the Law Society of England and Wales and the General Council of the Bar, which may make it difficult for you to become a member of the legal profession in later life. It is consequently important that you cite all your sources fully and accurately. In addition, good referencing may gain you marks.

6.2: WHAT IS PLAGIARISM?

> Plagiarism is taking (some would say *stealing*) others' words OR ideas without stating whose words or ideas they are and where they came from.
>
> It is not just a case of failing to put quotation marks round someone else's words.
>
> It includes taking others' ideas, ones that you have not come up with yourself, and then not stating that they belong to someone else.
>
> Paraphrasing others' words is only acceptable if you attribute those ideas to the person who thought of them.

In other words you should cite the other person's work if:

- You are quoting their words.

- You are paraphrasing their words by using their ideas but not their exact words (any ideas that you have not come up with yourself).

To be clear, plagiarism is taking someone else's words or someone else's ideas without stating the sources from which you got them. This would include taking a chunk of text from a book or an electronic source including the internet, and putting it in your essay without putting quotation marks around the words and without putting a footnote stating the source of those words. It would include putting someone else's words into your own words (called paraphrasing) and not putting a footnote stating from where these ideas originated. Students often say that they find it hard to know when to put a reference or footnote to another's source. The rule of thumb should be that you put a reference or footnote whenever you have not come up with the idea you are discussing or the words you are using yourself. This means that most paragraphs will contain a number of references or footnotes to others' work, although it is likely that the first sentence and last sentences are your own original work and will thus not need to be referenced/footnoted.

6.3: HOW TO REFERENCE

There are different ways of citing work; however, there are certain key pieces of information that a full reference must contain.

Adopt a consistent style and make sure you include all the relevant information.

Learn to use footnotes or endnotes if you have not used them before.[5]

There are some general rules about how you should display case names, statutory references and quotes from texts. Many of the rules are not hard or fast, but you do need to adopt a consistent style throughout your answer. Try to find a

---

5 A footnote generally appears at the bottom of the page as this one does and contains all the information that is necessary for the reader to find the original source. Word processing programmes such as Word have an 'add footnote' function in the 'insert' menu on the toolbar.

style that suits you, make sure it conforms to any guidelines you have been given by your tutors, and then stick to it. The general rules are set out below.

6.4: HOW TO REFERENCE BOOKS

> **Author, initials, *Title of the book*, Edition (Place of Publication: Publisher, Year of publication), page number if relevant.**
>
> **For example:**
>
> **Webley, L. C., *Legal Writing* 2nd edn (London: Cavendish Publishing, 2009).**
>
> **Or**
>
> **Webley, L.C., (2009) *Legal Writing* 2nd Edition (London: Cavendish Publishing).**

A full reference for a book will include the name of the author, the title of the book, the edition of the book (if there is one), the place of publication of the book, the name of the publisher and the year of publication. This is enough information for the bibliography, but you will also need to provide a page reference for the source of your information in a footnote or endnote.

6.5: HOW TO REFERENCE JOURNAL ARTICLES

> **Author, initials, 'Title of the article' Volume number/year *Journal title* page reference.**
>
> **For example:**
>
> **Webley, L.C. 'Pro Bono and Young Solicitors: Views From the Front Line' Vol. 3 (2) (2000) *Legal Ethics* 152–168.**
>
> **Or**
>
> **Webley, L.C. (2000) 'Pro Bono and Young Solicitors: Views From the Front Line' Vol. 3 (2) *Legal Ethics* 152–168.**

A full reference for a journal article will include the name of the author, the title of the article (usually in quotation marks), the volume number and/or the year of the journal that the article appears in, the title of the journal and the start and end pages of the journal article. A full reference in a footnote would also include a reference to the page from which you have taken the idea or the quotation.

6.6: HOW TO REFERENCE CASES

> *Name of the case* (in full) (year) volume of the law report, Law Report
> abbreviations page reference.
> For example:
> *Attorney-General v. Guardian Newspapers Ltd (No. 2)* [1990] 1 AC 109
> Or
> <u>Attorney-General v. Guardian Newspapers Ltd (No. 2)</u> [1990] 1 AC 109

Cases should be either **bold**, or *italicised* or <u>underlined</u>. If you are writing by hand then they should be underlined. They should be written out in full if you are writing an assessment under anything other than exam conditions. If you are writing an answer to a problem question in an exam and you have not been permitted to bring materials such as a notebook in with you, then use of abbreviated forms of case names is usually acceptable. <u>Do not put the full case reference in the text. If you wish to cite the case reference then put it in a footnote or an endnote.</u> An example of a case name displayed in traditional form would be as set out above. The 'v.' should have a full stop after it to indicate that it is an abbreviation. It is pronounced in speech in UK legal circles as 'and' and not 'versus'. Square brackets are often put around the year that the case was reported, if there is no volume number in that series of law reports. Round brackets are usually used if there is a volume number. However, this is not always the case, as indicated in the example above, as some law reports have conventions particular to that series.

6.7: HOW TO REFERENCE STATUTES

> The full name of the Act including the year of enactment plus the sections
> to which you refer.
>
> Human Rights Act 1998 s. 1 (indicating section 1)
> Human Rights Act 1998 ss. 1–6 (indicating sections 1–6)

Statute names should be displayed in full the first time you use them, but as long as you provide a definition, they may then be cited in abbreviated format thereafter. Remember that it is important to cite the year in the full citation, as there may be a number of statutes that have the same short title but were passed in different years and this may make all the difference. Statute names should be in title case – the first letter of each word should be captialised – and may be in **bold**, *italicised*, or <u>underlined,</u> if you prefer.

An example of a statute displayed in traditional form is set out above. If you wish to use an abbreviation for all subsequent mentions of the Act then please define the abbreviation when you provide the full citation as so:

Human Rights Act (HRA) 1998, thereafter cited as HRA 1998.

Remember too that whenever you refer to the 'Act', the 'A' should be capitalised thus:

The Act came into force on the 2nd October 2000.

If you are citing particular sections of an Act then you may write 'section' or abbreviate that to 's.'.

'The Human Rights Act 1998 s. 6 states that . . .'

If you are referring to multiple sections then you would cite them by doubling the 's':

'The Human Rights Act 1998 ss. 6–8 indicates that . . .'

If you are unsure then it is always safer to go with the long version, to write out the word 'section' than to make up an abbreviation.

6.8: HOW TO REFERENCE WEB PAGES

> **Web citations should follow the conventions above for either books or articles; however, they should also include the web page address at which they may be accessed and also the date on which the page was accessed (as content changes on the web).**
>
> **Syrett, K. 'Of resources, rationality and rights: emerging trends in the judicial review of allocative decisions.' [2000] 1 *Web JCLI* at http://webjcli.ncl.ac.uk/2000/issue1/syrett1.html accessed on 25th June 2004.**

Web page citations follow the citation conventions set out for books or articles for the first part of the citation, but then also include a full reference to the web page at which the article can be found as well as the date on which you accessed it. You should include the date as web page content is dynamic and changes rapidly. Errors could have been corrected since you accessed the page, or alternatively the article could have been replaced or removed altogether. By including the date you are more protected from the charge that you have incorrectly cited information.

6.9: HOW TO REFERENCE EDITED COLLECTIONS

These are a hybrid of journal articles and book citations as follows:
Author of the chapter, Initial, 'Title of chapter' Editors name, initial (eds) *Title of Book* (Place of publication: Publisher, Year) pages of the chapter.
For example:
McGlynn, C. 'Judging Women Differently: Gender, The Judiciary and Reform' in Millns, S. and Whitty, N. (eds) *Feminist Perspectives on Public Law* (London: Cavendish Publishing, 1999) pp 87–106
Or
McGlynn, C. (1999) 'Judging Women Differently: Gender, The Judiciary and Reform' in Millns, S. and Whitty, N. (eds) *Feminist Perspectives on Public Law* (London: Cavendish Publishing) pp 87–106

Edited collections are hybrids of journal article and book citations. You should include the name of the author of the chapter, the title of the chapter in quotation marks, the names of the editors, the title of the book in italics, the place of publication, the publisher and the year of publication. Footnoted sources should also include the page number from which the source originates.

6.10: HOW TO REFERENCE OTHERS' REFERENCES

You must cite all sources of information including the source that your source is citing.

If your source refers to someone else's source then cite both:

For example:
Dicey (1885), p 39 as cited in Barnett, H. *Constitutional and Administrative Law* 7th edn (London: Routledge-Cavendish, 2008) at p 133.

In the example, Barnett is my source but I want to refer to Dicey to whom Barnett refers and cites in her work.

To avoid a charge of plagiarism you must be sure to cite your sources (the book or article that you have read) as well as the source of the original information. This sounds to be complicated but is actually quite easy. Your source is your reference point and the reader needs to know from where you got the information. The source of the original information is the source that your textbook writer or other author mentions. Your footnote needs to include all the information required to find the original source and your source. That way the reader may retrace your research steps and also those of the people who have done their own research to find the original source of the information.

6.10.1 USING ABBREVIATIONS IN FOOTNOTES AND ENDNOTES

Students tend to get rather worried about how to use Latin abbreviations in footnotes. The honest answer is that you can get away with English equivalents in many cases, but if you do want to use the traditional form of footnote and endnote abbreviations, this is how to do it.

Always write out the reference in full the first time you refer to an author's work. You may thereafter abbreviate the reference. There are conventions on how to do this, although there are a number of different options to choose from. Whichever you choose, make sure that you use the same style throughout your assessment. Academics tend to prefer to use Latin abbreviations instead of English ones. Abbreviations should always end with a full stop as indicated below, although in more modern texts full stops are omitted to provide a less cluttered style. Useful abbreviations include:

Latin abbreviations

Latin abbreviations you may see during your research and reading, and which you may use in your essays, are:

Id.

Ibid.

Loc. cit.

Op. cit.

Supra

Id. – This means 'exactly the same as cited directly above' and is used if the footnote or endnote is exactly the same as the one immediately above it. It should be the same in all respects including the same page reference. In this instance the footnote would simply contain the abbreviation 'id.' Or 'Id.'. Many people do not use 'Id.' but instead now use 'Ibid.' instead.

Ibid. – This means 'in exactly the same book as cited directly above' and is used if the footnote or endnote is exactly the same as the one immediately above this one, but for a different page number. In this instance the footnote would be displayed thus:

1. Sherr, A.H. and Webley, L.C., 'Legal Ethics in England and Wales' (1997) Vol. 4 Nos. 1/2 *International Journal of the Legal Profession* pp 109–138.
2. *Ibid.* at p 130, or *Ibid.* at 130, or *Ibid.* p 130.

Loc. cit. – This means 'in the place that has been cited above' and is used where the full citation for a book, report or journal article has been provided previously in an earlier footnote of endnote, including the page reference or the paragraph. It is similar to '*id.*' but for the fact that there are other footnotes or endnotes in between the original citation and the current one. In traditional works this form of abbreviation is not used for cases or for legislation, which should be cited in full in each instance; however, the rule is becoming blurred.

3. Sherr, A.H. and Webley, L.C., *loc. cit.* at note 1.

Op. cit. – This means 'in the work cited above' and is used where the full citation has been provided in an earlier footnote or endnote above, but not in the footnote immediately above this one. *Op. cit.* relates to books, reports and journal articles but not to cases or to legislation. In order for the reader to know which source the writer refers to, the footnote should also contain the authors of the source and may include the footnote or endnote that contains the full citation as follows:

4. Sherr, A. H. and Webley, L. C., *op. cit.* at note 1 at p 131.

This could be displayed in a more simplified form as follows:

4. Sherr and Webley, *op. cit.* at 131, or 4. Sherr and Webley, *op. cit.* at p 131.

Supra – This means 'above' and is used where the full citation has been provided previously in an earlier footnote or endnote. It would normally be followed by the footnote number that contains the full citation as well as the page number relevant to the current footnote. *Supra* is often used in essays in place of both *loc. cit.* and *op. cit.*

There are others, but these are the most commonly used in legal academic writing.[6] An English equivalent to the Latin versions would simply be to write 'As above' followed by the identifying information that follows the Latin abbreviations in the examples above.

---

6 For a fuller discussion of Latin abbreviations and their use in footnotes and endnotes see Campbell, E. and Fox, R., *Students' Guide to Legal Writing and Law Exams* 2nd edn (Sydney: The Federation Press, 2003).

6.11: BIBLIOGRAPHIES VS. FOOTNOTES/ ENDNOTES

A bibliography is used at the end of a piece of legal writing. It sets out all the sources to which you personally referred.

Footnotes appear at the bottom of each page and they contain the sources you referred to as well as any sources that you are referring to which your own source also referred to (as set out above).

Endnotes are similar to footnotes but they all appear at the end of the piece of legal writing, although they are numbered in the text in ways similar to footnotes.

Some lecturers may ask you to use footnotes, or to use endnotes. Some will require you to include a bibliography of your sources at the end of your writing as well as footnotes/endnotes; others will not require both. Check to see what the conventions are for each module.

To conclude, it is important that you reference your work fully. If in doubt, it is better to over-reference rather than to under-reference. Keep clear notes of your sources during the research phase including the page numbers from which you have taken notes. It is often easier to photocopy the title page of the source you are using at the same time as you photocopy the pages to which you are going to refer, as this contains most of the information that you will need for your footnotes. Your bibliography will include all sources that you have read and made use of in your written work.

Next steps:

• Check your written work carefully to make sure that you have either properly quoted or properly paraphrased others' work.

• Any idea or phrase that is not your own, should be cited appropriately.

• Check too that you have properly referenced all your sources according to the Harvard or the Oxford methods of referencing (or your law school's own style).

• Check your bibliography to make sure that you have included any source that has helped to form your views in writing the answer. Do not include sources that you have not read personally.

- There are also some exercises to undertake to test your ability to reference and cite others' work, which you may wish to try. The answers are towards the back of the book.

- There are further exercises on citing and referencing on the companion website.

- You may wish to check your understanding of the difference between quoting and paraphrasing by visiting the companion website where you can test your knowledge.

6.12: TEST YOUR UNDERSTANDING OF REFERENCING: CITING OTHERS' WORK

Read the extract below from Hilaire Barnett's book then try the following task. There are answers set out at the back of the book.

'6

PARLIAMENTARY SOVEREIGNTY [7]

. . .

INTRODUCTION

[1] Under any constitution – whether written or unwritten – there must be a source of ultimate authority: one supreme power over and above all other power in the state. Under a written constitution the highest source of power is the Constitution as interpreted by the Supreme Court. Under the British constitution, in theory if not in practice, the highest source of authority is the United Kingdom Parliament and Acts of Parliament are the highest form of law.

---

7 Extract from Barnett, H. *Constitutional and Administrative Law* 7th edn (London: Routledge-Cavendish, 2009) pp 133–135.

[2] Writing in the late nineteenth century, A.V. Dicey took the view that the supremacy of Parliament is 'the dominant characteristic of our political institutions'.[8] However, the concept of sovereignty has long caused controversy and is one which assumes differing interpretations according to the perspective being adopted. For example, international lawyers are concerned with the attributes which identify a state as independent and sovereign within the international *[page 134 begins here]* community. Political scientists on the other hand are concerned with the source of political power within a state. From the perspective of legal theorists and constitutional lawyers the focus is on the ultimate legal power within a state.

To categorise Britain as a sovereign independent state with the ultimate source of legal authority vesting in its Parliament was accurate in the nineteenth century. However, in today's world of increasing economic legal and political interdependence the traditional theory of sovereignty has an air of unreality about it. International relations and obligations, membership of the European Union, devolution of law-making powers away from Westminster to Northern Ireland, Scotland and Wales and other factors all restrict what Parliament can in fact do: theory and practice are increasingly separated. In this chapter we examine the various aspects of sovereignty, and the challenges posed to the orthodox view.

DIFFERING INTERPRETATIONS OF 'SOVEREIGNTY'

Political and legal sovereignty – from the standpoint of sovereignty within the state as opposed to sovereignty as understood in international law – may be analysed as meaning either the supreme legal authority within a state or the supreme political authority within a state.[9]

SOVEREIGNTY AS SUPREME LEGAL AUTHORITY

It is this interpretation with which A.V. Dicey and later constitutional writers are concerned. As this meaning is the central focus of our concern in understanding legislative – or parliamentary – sovereignty, consideration will be postponed until other interpretations of the concept have been considered.

SOVEREIGNTY AS SUPREME POLITICAL AUTHORITY

The essence of this idea is that lawful power and authority must be in conformity with moral dictates: some form of 'higher law' or 'natural law'. Political

---

8 Dicey, 1885, p 39.
9 For a more elaborate categorisation, see Rees, 'The theory of sovereignty restated', in Laslett, 1975, Chapter IV.

theorists of the eighteenth century contributed much to an understanding of the idea of ultimate authority. Four broadly similar approaches, each entailing the idea of a 'social contract', may be outlined here.

[3] Thomas Hobbes[10] offered the most extreme version of the social contract theory, arguing that man by nature is incapable of regulating his life in peace and harmony with his fellow man. Hobbes's view of man in a society lacking a restraining all-powerful sovereign was inherently pessimistic, an attitude encapsulated in the often quoted phrase that life is 'solitary, poor, nasty, brutish and short'. In order for there to be civil order, it was necessary for each man to surrender to the state his own sovereignty in exchange for security. Such a surrender was revocable only if the state abused its trust. The requirement of obedience to law is strict; and yet there are limits: *[page 135 begins here]*

> If the Sovereign command a man (though justly condemned) to kill, wound, or mayme himselfe; or not to resist those that assault him; or to abstain from the use of food, ayre, medicine, or any other thing, without which he cannot live; yet hath that man the Liberty to disobey.

Further, Hobbes states that:

> The Obligation of Subjects to the Soveraign, is understood to last as long, and no longer, than the power lasteth, by which he is able to protect them. For the right men have by Nature to protect themselves, when none else can protect them, can by no Covenant be relinquished.

. . . '

1   Read the first paragraph marked with a [1] and quote the first sentence. Provide a full reference in a footnote for the quote.
2   Read the paragraph marked with [2]. Put the main points in your own words (paraphrase them) in one paragraph of your own, as you would for an essay. Provide footnotes citing that work in full.
3   Read the paragraph marked with [3] and quote Barnett's first quotation including the lead-in sentence. Provide a full reference including the primary and secondary source.

The answers are set out in the answer section towards the end of the book.

---

10 *The Leviathan*, 1651.

6.13: REFERENCING EXERCISE TWO: FULL AND ACCURATE REFERENCING

Look at the following title pages and then write a full citation for each one. The answers are towards the back of the book.

FEMINIST PERSPECTIVES ON PUBLIC LAW

Cavendish
Publishing
Limited

London and Sydney

First published in Great Britain 1999 by Cavendish Publishing Ltd,
The Glass House, Wharton Street, London WC1X 9PX, United Kingdom
Telephone: +44 (0) 171 278 8000   Facsimile: + 44 (0) 171 278 8080
E-mail: info@cavendishpublishing.com
Visit our Home page on http://www/cavendishpublishing.com

Feminist perspectives on public law
1.   Public law
II. Millns, S II. Whitty, Noel
342.4'1

ISBN 1 85841 480 X

Printed and bound in Great Britain

Extract from Contents Page:

cont . . .

Cite in full Thérèse Murphy's chapter in this edited collection.

CONSTITUTIONAL & ADMINISTRATIVE LAW

················ SEVENTH EDITION ················

Hilaire Barnett

Routledge-Cavendish

Seventh edition first published 2009
by Routledge-Cavendish
2 Park Square, Milton Park, Abingdon, Oxon OX14 4RN

Simultaneously published in the USA and Canada
by Routledge-Cavendish
270 Madison Ave, New York, NY 10016

*Routledge-Cavendish is an imprint of the Taylor & Francis Group,
an informa business*

© 2009 Hilaire Barnett

First five editions published by Cavendish Publishing Limited
First edition 1995
Second edition 1998
Third edition 2000
Fourth edition 2002
Fifth edition 2004
Sixth edition 2006

Typeset in Adobe Garamond and Helvetica Neue by
RefineCatch Limited, Bungay, Suffolk
Printed and bound in Great Britain by
MPG Books Ltd, Bodmin, Cornwall

British Library Cataloguing in Publication Data
A catalogue record for this book is available from the British Library

Library of Congress Cataloging in Publication Data
Barnett, Hilaire.
   Constitutional & administrative law / Hilaire Barnett. – 7th ed.
      p. cm.
   Cover title: Constitutional and administrative law
   Includes bibliographical references and index.
   1. Constitutional law – Great Britain.   2. Administrative law – Great
   Britain.   I. Title.   II. Title: Constitutional and administrative law.
   KD3989.B374 2008
   342.41 – dc22   2008006790

ISBN10: 0–415–45829–3 (pbk)
ISBN13: 978–0–415–45829–0 (pbk)

Cite Hilaire Barnett's book in full as you would in a bibliography.

SUMMARY

Others' words and ideas must be fully and accurately referenced in your written work. Failure to reference properly may result in marks being deducted for poor scholarship, or a charge of plagiarism being made against you.

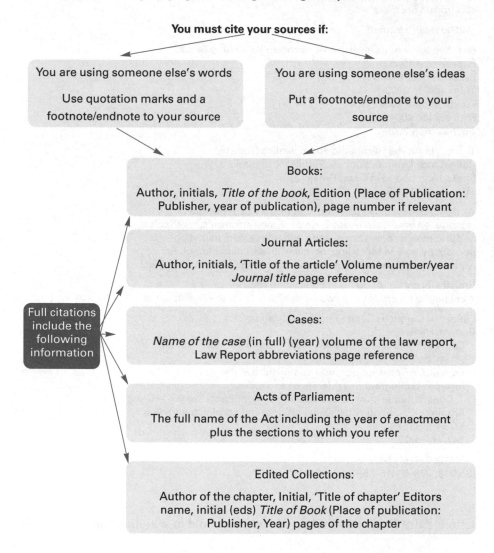

You must cite your sources if:

You are using someone else's words

Use quotation marks and a footnote/endnote to your source

You are using someone else's ideas

Put a footnote/endnote to your source

Books:

Author, initials, *Title of the book*, Edition (Place of Publication: Publisher, year of publication), page number if relevant

Journal Articles:

Author, initials, 'Title of the article' Volume number/year *Journal title* page reference

Full citations include the following information

Cases:

Name of the case (in full) (year) volume of the law report, Law Report abbreviations page reference

Acts of Parliament:

The full name of the Act including the year of enactment plus the sections to which you refer

Edited Collections:

Author of the chapter, Initial, 'Title of chapter' Editors name, initial (eds) *Title of Book* (Place of publication: Publisher, Year) pages of the chapter

7 COMPLETING, POLISHING AND PRESENTING YOUR WORK

Essays and problem question answers are not just about the ideas that are contained within them, although they are obviously extremely important. They are also about communicating those ideas and the evidence you have to back up your assertions in an effective and stylish fashion. The way in which you communicate those ideas will make it easier or harder for you to persuade the reader around to your way of thinking. The more gaps you leave in your arguments, and the less clearly you express your ideas, the more likely it is that you will lose the reader and the chance to get your point across. This chapter considers the important stage of finishing and polishing your answer before handing it in to be marked. It provides some hints to help you make the most of your writing.

7.1: FINISHING AND POLISHING YOUR WRITTEN WORK

Finish the first draft of your essay.

Leave it alone for 24 hours.

Return to your essay.

Read the draft to check it as a whole.

Reread the question or problem and then reread your draft once through.

Take note of the ideas and arguments in the draft.

Start at the beginning and ask yourself:

• 'Have I answered the question?'

• 'Do I need to rearrange the order of ideas so that they flow?'

- 'Have I explained where my arguments are going throughout the essay?'

- 'Have I grouped together ideas that point in one direction?'

Make any changes.

Read the draft again to check individual paragraphs.

Ask yourself for each paragraph:

- 'Have I stated the point I am making?'

- 'Have I explained my point?'

- 'Have I provided evidence to back up the point?'

- 'Have I cited all my sources?'

- 'Have I rounded off the point by explaining its relevance to the question?'

Reread one final time to check that:

- **Your spellings and grammar are correct.**

- **Your essay looks professional.**

It is difficult to reflect on your own work, and particularly if you complete your first draft and then move to polish and finish it straight away. Leaving a period of 24 hours between completing your draft and starting to polish it will allow the issues to settle in your mind. It will also make it easier to view your essay objectively, to read it as the marker will read it. Students tend to lose 'easy' marks by failing to polish their work. Spelling errors are avoidable (although I'll leave you to spot how many you can find in this book!) as are formatting problems, missing footnotes, poor editing mistakes. Just for fun, an example that would not be atypical would be something like this:

> *'Parliamentary supremmacey is a theory of how what power Parliament has to legislate. . . theorists such as Dicy have set out the basic tennents of the theory.[1]'*

While the ideas contained in those two sentences would give a student some marks, they may equally have resulted in a drop of overall essay mark, because the essay was so badly finished. In addition, the citation is missing and the point is not fully made.

1

7.1.1 LINKING IDEAS INTO AN ARGUMENT

Once you have written your essay or your problem question answer, it is important that you read through your draft. You may have assigned one paragraph per idea and you may have explained how the idea related to the question; however, it is difficult to link each of the ideas together in your essay at the same time as writing them down for the first time. Most students, and indeed many academics, do not know what they think about a subject until they have either discussed the ideas or written them down. Consequently, it is hard to develop and link ideas at the point when you are trying to get them down on paper. Instead, it is important to give yourself a break from your essay once the first draft is completed, to let the ideas settle in your mind for a day or so, and then to return to your draft to link those ideas together in your essay.

Linking ideas is simply a way of explaining how one idea fits with the next, so that the reader can develop a picture of how the ideas relate to one another. One of the easiest ways of doing this is to group those issues that appear to point to one answer in your essay, for example, issues that appear to be in favour of a proposition in a title, and those that appear to be against a proposition. Alternatively, you may wish to adopt a thematic approach. You may wish to balance one paragraph, which argues in favour of one point of view, with a following paragraph that appears to contradict it, before moving on to the next theme on your list. There are many different ways to link ideas, but the important part of argument construction is that the reader can follow the development of your ideas, rather than that you adopt a particular pattern.

Problem question answers should be structured so as to move logically through the legal issues that must be proved or disproved, met or not met, in order for the legal points to be settled. Some legal issues are prerequisites and if these have not been met then the client may have no case at all. For example, a judicial review case cannot be brought if a client cannot demonstrate that the body that carried out the act, omission or made the decision that is the subject of the dispute, falls within the definition of a public body or a public authority. A problem question answer should address this issue early on, as if it cannot be proved, the client will have no case regardless of whether the other legal and factual issues can be proved. Take your lead from the general principles of law that govern the legal situation that is the subject of the problem.

Once you are sure that you have linked your ideas and that together they answer the question, then the final stage is to check your draft for spelling, grammar, footnotes and formatting issues.

7.1.2 GRAMMAR AND PUNCTUATION

Grammar worries most people a little bit and many of us a lot. It is one of the things that crops up time and time again in student feedback from assessments. Grammatical issues are not quite the same as stylistic ones – people adopt different styles of writing but sentences do need to be grammatically correct, if they are to be understood. You are encouraged to adopt your own style of writing, within certain limits, but you do need to adhere to the basic rules of grammar. If you are unsure about punctuation issues you may wish to read *Eats Shoots and Leaves*[2] which is a humorous and practical guide to punctuation, which has also become a best seller. If you are really worried about your English grammar then you may either decide to make use of a grammar book or to ask your personal tutor about English grammar and writing courses run by the university. Most universities do have very good 'writing for academic success' and 'English for academic purposes' courses for undergraduate and postgraduate students and it may be as well to do the course towards the beginning of your degree, even if it means dropping a law option, rather than struggling with grammar issues throughout your studies. Apart from anything else, your grades will likely be much improved, if you undertake such a course. There are some general rules that I shall mention here.

You must write in fully formed sentences, even if you are in a hurry and even if there is a much funkier way of writing the sentence in txt format. Surprising though it may sound, essays are occasionally submitted in which 'you' has become 'U' and 'to' has become '2'. Funny though this is, this style does not achieve good marks for a student in an assessment unless the marker has a particularly odd sense of humour.

- Sentences must begin with a capital letter.
- Sentences must end with a full stop.
- Any words that are being quoted, where the words belong to someone else and not to the student, must be in quotation marks and must also be referenced.
- Capital letters should only be used in the middle of a sentence for proper nouns or for abbreviations (assuming these have been defined earlier in the written work) or for other defined words.
- Check to see whether you are using a plural or a possessive. There are a couple of words that trip up some students:

'It is' when shortened becomes 'it's' with an apostrophe. An apostrophe is not used for 'its' when it is used to explain that the thing in question

---

2 Truss, L. *Eats Shoots and Leaves. The Zero Tolerance Approach to Punctuation* (London: Profile Books, 2003).

belongs to 'it'. An example would be: *'Parliament has the power to self-regulate. Its power derives from parliamentary privilege.'*

- Words such as Parliament, Government, the Judiciary are usually referred to in the singular rather than the plural and so 'the Government is considering' is more usual than 'the Government are', although there are differences of opinion on this.
- Check that you have not put down the wrong spelling of words that sound the same. Examples include: their and there; weather and whether, two and too and to.
- Each new idea should be discussed in a new paragraph, and in a single paragraph. In other words do not start a new line for each new sentence.
- Words such as 'since' and 'while' can be difficult to use correctly. It is usually considered better practice to begin a sentence with 'Although it could be suggested that . . .' rather than 'Since' or 'While', although some people argue that this is a matter of style rather than grammar.
- Spellcheck your work.

Many of us feel that we need more help with our grammar. Consider using a grammar book to assist you in your writing to begin with and with luck you will find that your grammar gradually improves throughout your course. If you feel that you need extra help then ask your tutor whether there is a workshop or a module at your university that will help you to develop your writing skills.

7.1.3 STYLE ISSUES

Style is a personal thing, and written style is no different. However, there are conventions about the style you should adopt in writing an essay or an answer to a problem question. The conventions include whether the writer should write in the active or passive voice and whether to refer to third parties as 'him' or 'her' or 'them'. Different types of written work require different styles of writing. This book has been written in a relatively informal style, making use of 'you' and 'I' to communicate skills techniques to you in, what I hope is, a clear way in the form of conversation. This style may also be appropriate for a reflective essay, in which you reflect on your skills development. Nonetheless, grammar and punctuation rules still apply. However, most essays and problem question answers should adopt a style more similar to that seen in traditional textbooks, journal articles and cases. Formal written style is less personal and more distanced.

Problem questions are forms of professional writing, to a certain extent. They are a mode of communicating a professional opinion to another professional. These tend to be written without reference to *'you'* or *'I',* but instead use phrases such as *'it is considered that . . .'* rather than *'I consider'* or *'I think'*. This adds authority to the opinion, as it makes the decision appear to be one that has been arrived at after professional deliberation. It gives it the aura of a professional rather than a personal decision. The more formal style provides extra gravity and distance and thus adds authority to it.

Essays and answers to problem questions are usually written in the passive voice. An example of the passive voice and the third person would be:

> Parliamentary supremacy has been examined to establish whether supremacy has been eroded as a result of the UK's membership of the EU.

An example of a similar sentence written in an active voice and in the first person would be:

> I am considering whether the UK's membership of the EU has eroded Parliamentary supremacy.

This second example shows two of the stylistic concerns that tutors may have with students' work. The convention is that written assessments are written in the third person and the passive. There is no mention of *'I think'*, or *'My view is'*, or *'My opinion would be that'*. It may seem rather strange, but that is the way it is. The assessment is personal to you in that you have done the research and the reading, made the notes, dissected the question, planned it and written an answer, but what you find and therefore what you write is supposed to be universal rather than personal – you are, rightly or wrongly, supposed to have hit upon the truth, or at least a truth, backed up by evidence, rather than simply a personal opinion. Some tutors may prefer you to write in the first person, in which case follow their instructions, obviously, but it is more usual to be expected to write in the third person. This book breaks many of the conventions by writing directly to you, rather than writing to an impersonal audience, because it is trying to communicate directly with you. Generally it is more acceptable to write in an impersonal voice, to provide professional distance and some weight to the writing.

7.1.4 FORMATTING AND PRESENTATION ISSUES

Most coursework will have to be word-processed and, if you are not sure how to use a computer, then it as well to take the opportunity of free computing lessons at university as soon as possible in your university career. It may feel comforting to put this off, but it will place you under more pressure at the point when you have to write your assessments.

Appropriate presentation is usually one of the assessment criteria against which your essay or problem question will be judged. Markers will obviously expect far more from you in presentation terms as regards coursework, when you have the time to work on formatting and presentation, than for work written under exam conditions. Check to see whether your course has standard requirements for word-processed answers. If not, then you may wish to make use of the following:

- Case names should be underlined if handwritten, or italicised or in bold, or underlined if typed.
- Quotation marks are usually ' ', but may be " ". Some people use ' ' for the main quote and " " for quotes that come within the main quotes.
- Quotations are usually kept within a paragraph unless they are three or four lines long, in which case they may be put on a new line and indented from the left.
- Numbers are usually written in words for number one to nine and then in figures from 10 onwards.
- Phrases such as 'for example' should normally be written in full in the main body of an essay, but may be abbreviated to 'e.g.' in footnotes.
- Abbreviated words such as *'don't', 'won't', 'shouldn't'* should normally be written in full as *'do not', 'will not', 'should not'.*
- Footnote numbers usually come at the end of sentences and after punctuation.[3] It is not that important, but do adopt a consistent approach.
- Headings should also be consistent. In other words, make sure that headings of the same level (subheading one, for example) look the same throughout your essay. Adopt a different style of heading for the next level of headings down.

Once you have checked the presentation and formatting issues, you are ready to move on to the final checking change.

7.2: FINAL CHECKS

- Reread the question.

- Revisit any materials handed out with your assessment.

- Revisit any instructions you were given with the assessment including the word limit.

- Check the deadline date.

---

3   Unless you need to refer to more than one footnote in a sentence, in which case you may put a footnote number in the middle of a sentence, or unless the footnote relates to one point in a sentence that contains more than one point.

- Consider the assessment and grading criteria.

- Read through your essay one last time to check that it reads well, the references are complete and there are no typographical or spelling errors.

Word limit – you are unlikely to achieve a good mark if you have written well under the word limit as the word limit indicates the level of detail and analysis that you need to include in your answer. Answers that are too brief usually lack sufficient research evidence to back up the points being made. It is as well to go back through the research stages to ensure that you have found as much relevant material as possible, and then interweave it into your answer. It should also assist in providing depth and authority to your answer. Answers that are well over the word limit may also be penalised. It may be that you can cut down your answer by some simple editing. Is it possible for you to simplify any of your sentences? Could you summarise some of your arguments or cut out irrelevant facts from case descriptions? Try to pare down your paragraphs to the essentials. Could you shorten sentences by removing lots of extra clauses and adding a few full stops? It is often possible to reduce the length of a passage by simply removing superfluous words (such as 'simply' in this sentence). Check the word limit and the way it is calculated (are footnotes included in the limit for example?) with your lecturer.

Deadline date – you may be penalised quite substantially if you fail to meet the deadline.

Materials that have been handed out with the essay title – has your lecturer provided any other materials that you may need to refer to in order to answer the question fully?

Assessment and grading criteria – check how you are being assessed. Chapter 1 provides some assistance on what assessment and criteria mean regarding your writing.

Finally, make sure that you have handed your work in by the deadline. Many universities do not award a mark to work that has been handed in late, unless you are able to show extenuating or special circumstances. All your hard work may be wasted if you hand your work in late.

Next steps:

- Reread your written work.

- Check how well it flows. Do your arguments link?

- Does it answer the question?

- Does it meet the assessment guidelines in terms of format, length, etc.?

- How well does it read? Is the written English as it should be? Have you spellchecked your work?

- You may want to test your understanding of stylistic issues by undertaking the brief task at the end of the chapter. The answers are towards the end of the book.

- If you remain concerned about your standard of written English and you do not think that referring to a grammar book is likely to solve the problem, then see your personal tutor to ask whether there are any courses designed for undergraduate students that you may take at the university.

- You may wish to review the examples of good and poor practice on the companion website.

7.3: TEST YOUR UNDERSTANDING OF STYLE ISSUES

Rewrite the following sentences in an appropriate style for an essay:

1   *'I think that Parliamentary supremacy has been lost as a result of Britain joining the European Community.'*

2   *'The Factortame case played an important role in our understanding on the way in which European law must be interpreted by the courts. We now know that given a straight fight between British law and European law, European law will win.'*

3   *'We don't really know whether the Human Rights Act has been semi-entrenched within the British constitution, as no Parliament has yet attempted to repeal it. I think that Parliament would face a public outcry if it did try to repeal the Human Rights Act and so I believe that, in real terms, the Human Rights Act is really entrenched.'*

Read through a previous essay you have written. How does your writing style compare against the style you will adopt in future essays? What are the differences and how will your alter your written style in the future, if at all?

SUMMARY

By finishing and polishing your written work, you hope to pick up on gaps in your arguments, poor use of expression, spelling and formatting errors and missing footnotes. This stage always takes longer than you think, so allow at least 24 hours to complete this stage before handing work in to be marked.

Once you have completed your essay in draft:

Leave it alone for 24 hours

Return to your essay

Overview check: read the draft to check it as a whole

Reread the question or problem and then reread your draft once through

Take note of the ideas and arguments in the draft. Start at the beginning and ask yourself the following questions:

'Have I answered the question?'
'Do I need to rearrange the order of ideas so that they flow?'
'Have I explained where my arguments are going throughout the essay?'
'Have I grouped together ideas that point in one direction?'

Make any changes

Paragraph check: reread the draft again to check individual paragraphs

Read each paragraph and ask yourself the following questions:

'Have I stated the point I am making?'
'Have I explained my point?'
'Have I rounded off the point by explaining its relevance to the question?'
'Have I provided evidence to back up the point?'
'Have I cited all my sources?'

Make any changes

Check your spellings and grammar

Final checks: reread your draft one final time

Check presentation and formatting

Check all citations are full and accurate. Check bibliography

8 LEGAL WRITING IN EXAMS AND HOW TO PREPARE

Legal writing in exams is very similar to legal writing in coursework essays and problem-based coursework. Students still need to follow similar steps in the writing process; however, the nature of the exam will change the marker's expectations of a written answer. This chapter will take you through the different types of law exams and the way this will affect your essay and problem question answers.

8.1: TYPES OF LAW EXAMS

- **Unseen exams:** you do not see the paper or questions in advance.

- **Seen exams:** you are given the paper/questions in advance to prepare.

- **Closed-book exams:** you may not take materials into the exams.

- **Open-book exams:** you may take specified materials into the exams.

The majority of law exams are unseen exams, which means that you will not have the questions in advance. Seen exams are exams for which you have either been given some or all of the questions or the exam paper itself in advance. There are two other main permutations as well, which are that the exam will be a closed-book one, meaning that you will not be permitted to take any materials into the exam with you, or open-book, in which you will be permitted to take in some materials and to refer to them. You need to be clear on the type of exam you will be sitting and prepare accordingly.

8.2:   TYPES OF QUESTIONS

- **Multiple choice:** you are set a series of questions and have a choice of answers for each question. You select the most appropriate one (or other as stated on the paper).

- **Essay based questions:** you are given a title or a question and then asked to answer it in an essay format.

- **Problem questions:** you are given a factual scenario and you are asked to advise a client or clients on their legal position.

The paper may contain three main different types of questions: multiple-choice questions, essay-based questions and problem questions. Multiple-choice questions do not require a written answer, but the other two types of questions require an answer written in paragraphs and in full sentences, with evidence to back up the points that are being made. The legal writing steps remain the same for different types of exams, but your preparation for them should be a little different.

8.3:   DIFFERENT TECHNIQUES

You should adopt a different technique and type of preparation for different types of exam and different types of questions.

You need to develop different sets of skills to perform well.

But there are some similarities as well.

The keys to success are:

- Preparation;

- Know your paper;

- Sort out your timing;

- Spend time reading the paper.

Your preparation should always involve you looking through past exam papers for each exam you will sit. It is extremely important that you know whether your paper is to be seen or unseen, whether it will be open-book (and if so what materials you will be permitted) or closed-book. It is also important that you know the anatomy of the paper, for example the number of questions on the paper by comparison with the number you have to answer. You should also check whether you must answer particular questions or whether you have a completely free choice of questions on the paper. You should be clear on the length of time you have to write each answer, by dividing the total writing time available to you (this may be the same as the exam length, or slightly less if there is compulsory reading time as part of the exam) by the number of questions you must answer, assuming all questions are worth the same number of marks. That way, you narrow down the number of possible surprises during the exam. Most LLB or graduate diploma papers are relatively standard from year to year and thus it should be possible to be very well prepared before you enter the exam room.

Once you have entered the exam you should check that you have the correct paper in front of you and you should read the instructions on the front cover very carefully. A number of students fail exams unnecessarily each year, because they have not followed the instructions correctly and have answered too few or too many questions on the paper, or they have not answered a compulsory question. Once the exam starts, read through each question on the paper first, then return to the questions that you think you may answer and focus on those.

8.4: SIMILARITIES FOR ALL ESSAY AND PROBLEM QUESTION ANSWERS

> Dissect the question you have selected. Read it and then read it again. Many marks get wasted because students misread the questions or instructions.
>
> Plan your answer. Do not start writing straight away without planning.
>
> Check through your answers at the end if you have time, while checking the questions and instructions again.

You should approach your essay or problem question answer in the same way as you would outside an exam room, although you will be writing under timed exam conditions and consequently you will not have time to nip to the library to do any research, nor to write for as long as you would normally write for a piece of coursework. This actually makes your task much easier, rather than more challenging, believe it or not. If you have revised the topic that is the subject of the question and prepared for possible questions in advance, the writing process should be very straightforward. You should simply need to dissect the question and then jot down all the issues that you think may be relevant to answering it. Then note down any points that you need to make as regards each issue, put down any evidence to which you need to refer and consider how the issue relates to the question. Reread the question to make sure you are clear on your task, then begin writing. Follow the structure of the essay as set out below, if you are in any doubt about how to write an essay.

8.5: STRUCTURING AN ESSAY ANSWER

- **Make a list of relevant issues.**

- **Briefly jot down any evidence that relates to each issue.**

- **Organise your ideas into a logical order.**

- **Start writing.**

Structuring an essay answer:

- **Start with an introduction.**

- **Explain what the question is asking you to write about and which issues you will consider in order to answer it.**

Middle section of the essay:

- **Organise your ideas into paragraphs, one idea per paragraph.**

- **Start your paragraph by introducing the idea to the reader.**

- **Develop and discuss the issue.**

- **Back up what you are saying about the issue with evidence.**

- **Conclude the paragraph by explaining how or why the issue is relevant to the question.**

Conclusion:

- **Pull the issues together in the conclusion to come to a final answer to the question.**

- Do not go back through all the evidence.

- Do not introduce new ideas.

Problem question answers are not that different in structure, although the arguments you are advancing are a little different. Follow the structure for essay writing, but bear the following points in mind as you do so.

8.6: STRUCTURING A PROBLEM QUESTION ANSWER

Important: Who are you advising? All the parties or named individuals?

Remember that a good lawyer does not give a one-sided viewpoint.

Start off each paragraph by making the point rather than by pointing out the evidence for a point you have not yet made.

Therefore, do not start a paragraph with a discussion of the facts of a case. Cases are evidence of the law as stated in legislation or the common law. Make your point first, then use the case(s) to back it up.

Remember to advise your client; do not just talk about the general legal position.

A good lawyer does not give a one-sided legal opinion at this stage of a case. It is dangerous to ignore the possible legal pitfalls that the client may experience if the case were to come to court. You should be realistic about your client's chances. If there is case law that weakens your client's case then say so as well as providing case law that supports it. Angle your question towards your client's situation rather than writing an opinion on how the law stands on the legal topic that is the subject of the problem. You will not do well if you answer a problem question by providing an essay on the law of judicial review, for example. Instead, you should refer to your client's case in each paragraph and you should use cases and statutory references to back up the points you make, but not as a way of discussing the law in general terms.

8.7: LEGAL SOURCES

> You must provide evidence to back up your points in problem questions, and this is evidence that could be cited in court. Judges will generally only allow:
>
> - Primary and secondary legislation and common law (plus EU law and in some cases International law);
>
> - Cases from courts in England and Wales, which have precedent value. These will be binding according to the rules of precedent. These are evidence of how the law has been interpreted previously;
>
> - Some persuasive authorities from other common law jurisdictions with similar law may also be cited in support.

You must provide evidence to back up your points in problem questions and this evidence is evidence that could be cited in court. Cases that have precedent value are extremely important. The judgments from other cases in England and Wales that may not have a binding precedent authority may also be persuasive if they address the same point(s) of law as your client's case. The judgments of Commonwealth jurisdictions may also be persuasive in the same way as non-precedent cases above. No other sources are classed as 'legal sources'. Occasionally, academic texts are referred to as evidence of the law if there is no case law on the point or if the case law is terribly confused. Certain sections of *Hansard* may be referred to as an aid to the interpretation of legislation by judges.

8.8: MOST FREQUENT REASONS FOR FAILURE IN EXAMS

> - Did not answer the correct number of questions having misunderstood the instructions;
>
> - Ran out of time and did not answer the correct number of questions;
>
> - Did not answer the question set/misunderstood the question and answered one they made up themselves;

- **Wrote an essay on the general law rather than advising the client in a problem question;**

- **Had not looked at past papers before the exam and so did not know what to expect.**

Sometimes students fail exams because they do not know anything about the subject upon which they are being examined. More usually they fail because they have not demonstrated that knowledge in the right way by answering the correct number of questions set within the given time period. This is entirely avoidable if a student has prepared for an exam and has read the instructions properly before they start. Revision is an important part of the process, and the next section provides a revision structure you may wish to follow.

8.9: REVISION TECHNIQUES

- **You need to revise for an exam not for a subject.**

- **In other words, you must look at the past papers before you start your revision.**

- **Learning chunks of information will not get you a high mark for essay and problem questions, but may for multiple-choice exams.**

- **You need to be clear on the general principles for each topic that could be the subject of a question you will answer.**

- **You should revise by considering what the general principles of law are for a given topic.**

- **You then need to work out what evidence you have to back them up from cases, legislation and from academic opinion where the cases or legislation are not clear-cut.**

- **You need to be clear on how the topics fit together in the subject.**

There is little point in learning large chunks of information unless you are about to sit a multiple-choice exam. Essay and problem questions are set to test your understanding of the law and to make sure that you know the general principles of each topic on which you are examined. They are not a way to test how much law you can remember from your lectures. You should prepare for these types of essays by revising the general principles for each topic, as well as the evidence that supports the principles. You should also practise dissecting questions and working out which issues are relevant to them.

The easiest way to revise is as follows. Take a piece of paper and write the topic that you are revising at the top. The topics will have been set out in the module handbook or the lecture schedule. Next, read through your lecture notes, your textbook and other notes and make a list of issues that crop up within that topic. These are the general principles of the topic. Your list will look similar to the ones you have made at the planning stage of your essays and problem questions, although they will be more extensive. Write a sentence or a couple of sentences under each of the issues that are on your list, which explain the nature of the general principle. Add in the detail of the principle and add in any evidence that you have to back up these points. Again, this is similar to an essay plan or a problem question plan, but is much more detailed. You should now have notes on a topic on two sides of A4, including a list of topics (which are the general principles) with a brief explanation of each, followed by sub-issues for each topic and evidence to back them up. If you do not understand any aspect of the information you have on your sheet of paper then you should go back to your notes and reread that section. You will not be able to write a good essay if you do not understand the issues. Finally, you need to learn the information on the sheet.

 *Visit the Companion Website for an example of a revision sheet.

Once in the exam you will identify those questions that you will answer. After dissecting the question you can simply note down the general principles in a plan, one per paragraph and jot down the supporting information you can remember from your sheet of paper. Some of the principles from the sheet will not be relevant and those can be crossed out, some you may not remember; however, you will already have a basic essay or problem question plan prepared prior to the exam, which should take the pressure off you.

8.10: PREPARATION FOR OPEN-BOOK EXAMS

If you are allowed to take a notebook or folder in with you:

- Make sure you know the regulations for the notebook; for example, must it contain handwritten notes, be a certain size, etc.?

- Include as much useful material on the topic as possible including evidence to back up the points.

- Make sure you understand the information that is in there. The exam is not the best place to try to make sense of the topic.

- Organise the book so that you know where to find things as quickly as possible.

- Check whether you are permitted to highlight or underline materials.

Lecturers will expect more from your answer if you have access to information in a notebook, a statute book or a textbook in the exam. This means your answer should include more evidence to back up your points, as you will have access to that evidence rather than having to remember it as you would in a closed-book exam. There will be an expectation that you will have the general principles at your fingertips, plus cases and statutes and academic quotes.

You will need to spend time preparing your materials for the exam. Make sure that you know whether you are permitted to underline or highlight passages, or to write in books that can be taken in. If you get this wrong then, at best, your materials will be taken from you. There is little point having material with you that you cannot use in the exam. The more time you spend flicking through your books, the less time you have to write. Less generally means more in terms of notes or materials. It is better that you have fewer notes that are focused and which you can use, than that you arrive with three folders of material that you do not know at all. Index your materials if you can, and make sure that you have full citations for any sources that you will draw upon. The plagiarism rules will apply to any work that you cite from your notebook, so be sure to cite your sources.

Finally, the main theme of this chapter is preparation. It is relatively easy to do well if you know the types of question you will be asked, the time you have to write each answer and if you have revised the general principles, the evidence that backs them up and the way in which the general principles fit together. It is hard to do well if you enter the exam room unsure of what you have to do or how you will be tested. Prepare well and hopefully you will do well too. If, however, you find that you have not achieved the mark you expected, or you would hope for, ask for feedback from your tutor once you have your results. There are usually things that one can learn that will improve your marks for the future and there are very, very few students who cannot get through law exams with reasonable marks, because if we had doubts about your ability we probably would not have given you a place on the course in the first instance. Ask for feedback and use it as a way to improve your marks in the future. The next chapter provides some guidance on frequent feedback given to students to assist them to improve their performance.

> **Next steps:**
>
> - Read through the information in your module/course handbooks to check how you will be assessed in each module/course.
>
> - Make sure that you attend all revision lectures and tutorials and that you do any preparation that is required of you. These sessions are usually designed to give you useful feedback that will help your exam preparation.
>
> - Look through past papers for each module/course. Check how many questions you have to answer, of what type, how much choice you get and how long you have to answer each question.
>
> - Read through the assessment and grading criteria, if you can get hold of copies; if not, then refresh your memory of the generic grading criteria by rereading Chapter 1.
>
> Now begin your exam revision, in the light of your understanding of how you will be assessed.
>
> You may wish to look at the additional resources on the companion website to help with your legal writing technique in exams.

SUMMARY

The basic rules of revision technique are as follows:

You should revise for an exam not for a subject

| Refer to past papers in your law school before beginning revision | Target your revision to meet the requirements of the paper: open- or closed-book, multiple choice, essay questions or problem questions | Know how long you will have to write for each question, based on the marks to be awarded |

Begin revision

Target revision at the topics that have been covered in detail in lectures and tutorials, unless you have been told otherwise

You may wish to spend more time revising topics that occur frequently in past exam papers, although do so with care as syllabi do change from year to year

Multiple choice exams → Learn the detail from lecture, tutorial and textbook notes

Essay questions and problem questions
Closed-book exams
- Be clear on the general principles for each topic from lecture, tutorial and textbook notes. Learn the general principles
- Learn evidence in support of the general principles, including the ratio, not just the facts of the case
- Learn any evidence that limits the general principles, or adds exceptions to those principles

Essay questions and problem questions
Open-book exams
- Be clear on the regulations relating to the materials that can be taken into the exam
- Include as much useful material as possible on the possible topics, including evidence to back up the points
- Organise the book so that you know where to find things as quickly as possible
- Be clear on the general principles and include those in the notebook
- Include evidence in respect of the general principles

Once in the exam:

Check you have the correct paper

Read the instructions carefully to check how many questions you have to answer, whether there are compulsory questions, the time you have to write, etc

Read all the questions. Read them again and select those you are able to answer

Take each question you will answer in turn as follows:

• Make a list of relevant issues
• Briefly jot down any evidence that relates to each issue
• Organise your ideas into a logical order
• Start writing your answer

Follow the essay-writing guide in Chapter 2 to write an essay in paragraphs with an introduction, a middle section and a conclusion, with evidence to back up each point made

Take each question in turn. Do not spend longer on one question at the detriment of another

Check your work, if you have time

9 USING FEEDBACK TO IMPROVE PERFORMANCE

Lecturers find themselves writing similar comments on many of the essays and problem question answers they mark. It is not that they are churning out the same old comments, or at least that is generally not the case, but that the same issues keep cropping up in students' work. This book has attempted to show you how to make the most of your legal writing to achieve the highest possible marks, but if you find that you are receiving comments on the need to improve your essay structure, your focus in answering the question, your references and citations, use of bibliographies and your use of grammar, then the comments below may assist a little. Some of these explanations have been expanded in previous chapters. To make the most of your (admittedly limited) feedback opportunities, it is suggested that you do the following in conjunction with the feedback you have received:

1 Reread the assessment question and guidelines.

2 Reread the assessment and grading criteria.

3 Reread your assessed piece of work. How would you grade it? Why? What could you have done to improve?

4 Reread your feedback. How does that compare with your assessment of your written work? Do you need to talk to your tutor, or do you understand why you have received the mark and the comments that you have received?

5 Look back at your written work again. What relatively minor changes could have improved your work a good deal? What other modifications would take much more work?

6 What does this tell you about how you should approach future written work? How will you ensure that you build on your performance this time, so that you improve?

Reflection on one's performance is an integral part of the learning cycle and we miss out on good learning opportunities, if we give feedback only a cursory glance and then consign it to a folder or a drawer. There are relatively few opportunities for feedback on written work, so it is as well to make the most of those that are available. The next sections try to decode some of the feedback that you may see on your work.

9.1: COMMON FEEDBACK ON IMPROVING ESSAY STRUCTURE

- **Your written work should begin with an introduction that explains how you will approach the question.**

- **Your essay should be divided into paragraphs made up of sentences. Each paragraph should contain one main idea or issue. Paragraphs should follow on from each other and should be organised into an order that allows the ideas to develop into arguments. State the issue to be discussed at the beginning of each paragraph.**

- **A paragraph should begin with a sentence that sets out the idea or issue to be discussed within it. The middle section of the paragraph should discuss the issue and provide evidence in support of the discussion. Others' work should be referenced in footnotes or endnotes. The paragraph should then conclude by explaining the relevance of the issues to the question by stating what it means or why it is important as regards the question.**

- **Your essay should end with a conclusion that draws together the issues discussed in each paragraph, but which does not explain the detail of those issues. It should summarise them and provide a final answer to the question.**

All of these comments are about communicating ideas effectively to the reader. A well-structured essay allows the reader to follow the arguments put forward and to weigh up the evidence. A poorly structured essay may detract from the arguments, confuse the reader and appear to deviate from the question. A well-structured essay may contain the same content as the poorly constructed essay and yet the marks awarded would be very different. Communication is an important skill, and the structure of an essay will determine how well the ideas are communicated.

9.2: COMMON FEEDBACK ABOUT IMPROVING FOCUS TO ANSWER TO THE QUESTION

- You are marked on your ability to answer the question that has been set. You are not marked on your general understanding of the subject or the topic.

- You should spend some time analysing and dissecting the question to be sure that you understand the task that has been set. You may wish to rewrite the question in your own words or to make a list of the issues encompassed by the question.

- You should research the topics that are the subject of the question, by reading through your lecture and textbook notes and working out important themes. Then plan your research and your writing in the light of the question. Reread the question regularly to make sure that you are specifically addressing it.

- Make sure that you explain in your answer why and how each point you make is relevant to the question. If you cannot make a point relevant then do not include it.

This feedback relates to the student's ability to diagnose the problem set, or to dissect the question asked. The essay may be well structured, clearly written, well evidenced and presented and correctly referenced, but if it does not answer the question, the mark awarded will be towards the lower end of the spectrum. Students who have received this kind of feedback should spend longer on the diagnosis stage, by splitting up the question into the main topic and then the issues to be discussed, or dissecting the problem question into constituent facts, prior to researching the relevant law.

9.3: COMMON FEEDBACK ON CITATION/ REFERENCES AND BIBLIOGRAPHIES

- You must cite all the sources that you have referred to in your essay. This includes any words you have used from others' works or any ideas that you came across in others' works.

- You should cite sources in either footnotes or endnotes and you should retain a consistent style throughout your work.

- The reader should be able to look up each of the quotations or ideas you have referred to by taking the reference you have cited and using it to look them up. Citations must be full and accurate.

- If you refer to a source and find that you need to refer to the source that your source has cited, then you must cite both sources: your source (which will be the secondary source) and their source (the primary source).

- A bibliography should contain all the sources that you have drawn upon in the process of your writing. This will include all of your own sources that you cited in your footnotes (not primary sources from your secondary sources, however,) as well as other works that shape your ideas but which you have not directly cited in your footnotes/endnotes.

- A bibliography should be arranged in alphabetical order, usually by the authors' last names.

- You should group books under one heading, cases under another, etc., according to the range of sources to which you have referred. A good bibliography will include a range of sources.

- You should cite your sources in full.

The feedback is specific and relatively easy to put into practice in subsequent essays. Keep a full and accurate record of all sources to which you have referred in your research phase and follow the referencing conventions set out in Chapter 6. Proofread the essay or problem question answer before submitting it for assessment, to check that all footnotes are complete.

9.4: COMMON FEEDBACK ON SPELLING, PUNCTUATION, GRAMMAR AND STYLE

- You should check your written work to make sure that you have eliminated spelling errors and editing errors, as far as possible.

- You should read your work through to make sure that the sentences make sense.

- You are being assessed, in part, on your ability to communicate your ideas effectively, and poor grammar and poor spelling will detract from the ideas that you are trying to communicate. Most universities provide assistance with written English and so if you are concerned about your grammar then do talk to your personal tutor to find out what assistance there is within the university.

- Avoid using phrases that may be appropriate in everyday speech but that are not appropriate in written work, including slang, for example *'Dicey was like interested in the role of Parliament'.*

- Pay special attention to words that end in an 's', as these words may be plurals or they may be words that indicate that something belongs to someone or to something, for example: *'The students in the library.'* (Plural as there was more than one student in the library) *'The student's books were in the library.'* (One student had left her books in the library and the apostrophe indicates that the books in the sentence belonged to the student.)

- It is important that you check your work thoroughly before submitting it for assessment, as many errors are avoidable.

Most spelling errors are easy to correct using a spellcheck facility on the computer, assuming that the default language has been set correctly to 'English-British' rather than to 'English-US', for example. Many word-processing packages also have a grammar check facility, although these can be misleading, and consequently should be used with care.

Chapter 1 focuses on assessment and grading criteria and provides an analysis of what marks within different classifications mean in relation to student performance. Read through these again, if you are in doubt about what the mark you have been awarded means in respect of your own performance in an essay or problem question answer. A student who has been awarded a mark under 40% (assuming that 40% is the pass mark) needs to spend more time dissecting the question and getting to grips with the tasks. Once clear on the question, s/he should spend time reading through lecture and tutorial notes before carrying out research on the question. This should be translated into a plan and then into the essay, following the steps described in previous chapters. A student who has been awarded a mark of 40–49% has probably written an answer on the topic that is the subject of the question, but not on the question itself. A student who has been awarded a mark of 50–59% should concentrate on identifying the issues relevant to the question and using his or her research findings to construct an argument to answer the question. A student who has been awarded a mark of 60–69%, and who wishes to improve, should concentrate on developing his or her analysis of each issue by adding a sentence at the end of each paragraph, stating why and how the issue is relevant to the question, as well as undertaking further reading to provide depth to arguments within essays. A student who has been awarded a mark of 70% or more has done extremely well indeed; however, a student achieving 1st class marks should still review his or her performance, as there are always lessons to be learned. Plus, it is not always easy to replicate excellent marks in all subjects and so generic lessons are useful to transfer to other modules/courses and forms of assessment.

Essay writing technique tends to improve with practice. In addition, it also helps to read through the feedback from previous essays and then to refer to the question and the assessment criteria again to see whether you can learn from previous experience. It is also a good idea to reread your essay once you have received your mark and feedback, even though this can be a painful exercise. However, it is often possible to be able to see where one could improve, if the essay is reread along with the feedback. This is the best way to ensure that essay writing technique, and marks, improve in the future.

Next steps:

- Follow the steps at the beginning of this chapter for each piece of written work that you have had marked.
- Then consider feedback that you have received on previous written work. Do any common themes emerge?
- What do you need to do to improve your written work? How will you put this into practice? Do you need any further assistance from a tutor?

SUMMARY

Feedback provided by the marker is intended to help you to understand why you were awarded the mark given for the assessment. However, it is also a tool to assist you in improving your written work in the future. You should try to learn as much as you can from your previous performance, and use this to develop your approach, research, structure and written style in subsequent essays.

Before you undertake a piece of written work, look at previous feedback to remind yourself of potential pitfalls and how to avoid them in this work.

Once you have received feedback on your current essay, consider the following:

| Read through the feedback | Read through the assessment and grading criteria | Read through the question it seeks to answer |

Read through your answer and consider:

How far does your essay appear to provide a complete answer to the question? Have you included all relevant information? Have you included irrelevant information?

Have you made your points clearly? Will the reader know what point you have made in each paragraph?

Have you explained how your points relate to the question?

Do your arguments follow on from each other?

Have you provided authoritative evidence to back up all your assertions?

Have you provided full citations to all quotes and all ideas you have employed from others' work?

Reread the feedback. Does this accord with your views of your essay? If you are still unsure about what you could improve in the future, see your tutor to discuss it with him or her

Consider what you will do differently in future essays and problem question answers to improve your marks in subsequent written work

ANSWERS TO QUESTIONS

....

CHAPTER 1: APPLY YOUR KNOWLEDGE OF ASSESSMENT CRITERIA

'The British Parliament was once supreme.' Discuss with reference to Britain's membership of the EU and its obligations in relation to the European Convention on Human Rights.

> Identifies the main topic in issue in the question, which is good

> The sentence style needs a little work, and it is not usual to provide evidence or examples in the introduction. There was an attempt to outline the relevant issues to be discussed

This issue of parliamentary sovereignty has been that Parliament has been sovereign throughout centuries until the UK joined the European Community (European Communities Act 1972). Theorists such as Dicey have argued that Parliament is so powerful and so totally sovereign that it is allowed to do anything that it wishes, even to order that smoking on the streets of Paris could be outlawed by the UK Parliament. However, there are those who disagree with this and the essay will consider opinions for and against whether Parliament is supreme or not.

> Demonstrates that there are differing views and these will be considered, also good

> An attempt to set out the main topic and some of the issues that will be discussed in the essay. The introduction would have been even more powerful, if it had also signposted membership of the Council of Europe, and left the evidence on supremacy until the main body of the essay

This sentence does introduce, in relatively simplistic terms, the argument to be advanced. This is a good start, but there are ways of introducing the point in a more subtle way

This is a very general and forceful statement, without any evidence in support

Correct to an extent, although it may be helpful to note that this ECA 1972 is a British Act of Parliament, just as the writer states in a later paragraph in respect of the HRA 1998

It may be considered that sovereignty has been lost from Parliament. This is because Britain joined Europe and Europe's power overtook the power of the British Parliament. This was done through the enactment of the ECA 1972. Many are of the belief that the Act is now entrenched, that Parliament cannot repeal it. There was a recent case about this where a man wanted to weigh his fruit and vegetables in pounds and was told he could not because Europe says that we must all use kilogrammes and grammes. This shows that Parliament is no longer supreme.

Again, a general and forceful statement with no evidence in support. Who says so? Is their view authoritative and what is it based on?

The conclusion fits with what the student has said in the paragraph, which is good, but is not sufficiently nuanced given a proper reading of the evidence that s/he was trying to present

The student should have read the case – *Thorburn* – and if s/he had done this, the point would likely have been made more clearly. In addition, the ratio does not evidence the point being made

A good attempt at a fully developed paragraph, but the student does not appear to have read the evidence to which s/he refers and this pulls down the marks. The student also makes some sweeping statements without evidence to back them up

It would have been better to begin the paragraph without the use of the word 'however'. 'However,' tends to be used within a paragraph, but not at the beginning of a new paragraph. It may have been better to say something along the lines of 'There are commentators who consider, in contrast, that Parliament remains supreme even given membership of the EU.'

*However, there is a dispute about this point. The case of **British Railways Board v. Pickin** demonstrates that no Act of Parliament can be held to be invalid. This suggests that the courts must apply a British Act of Parliament and that Parliament can enact any law that it wishes; as long as the Act is passed it will become law in this country.*

This case is relevant evidence, but it would have been better to begin the sentence with the point being made, followed by the evidence in support. In addition, the evidence needed to be used in more detail, to illustrate the point, as a case name does not convey the legal principle that the case established in this regard. The marker may wonder whether the student has read the case

A reasonably good conclusion to the point being made, however, given the lack of detail in the sentence that preceded it, it is difficult for the reader to know whether it is accurate or not.

With a little more work, this could have been a good paragraph, assuming that more detail was provided and sources were cited fully and accurately

Useful evidence but the student needed to introduce the point to be discussed. It may have been better to add this sentence on to the paragraph above to allow the argument to be developed properly. The facts of the case are oversimplified and therefore not entirely correct. It would also have been better to explain the ratio of *Factortame (No. 2)* – the appropriate case – and then the importance of the ratio as regards the essay question

However, the **Factortame** case in the 1990s shows another side to this situation as the British courts did not apply the British Act of Parliament – the Merchant Shipping Act – but they applied the European law instead as they had been told they must by the European Court of Justice.

This is not really a full paragraph. The student should have developed a whole idea fully in a paragraph, and provided evidence in support of the idea, as well as a conclusion to the point being made. Also, it would have been better to avoid using the word 'however' after using it previously. Perhaps instead 'There are cases that appear to contradict this assessment, however . . .' would have been more appropriate

Not accurate. Parliament may legislate contrary to the ECHR, even though it would be a breach of the ECHR and the UK could be sanctioned by the ECtHR in international law. Consequently the conclusion that flows from that sentence is not correct. The student has confused the terms of the HRA 1998 with the ECA 1972. This suggests the student has not read the ECA 1972 or the HRA 1998. The student should have provided evidence in support of his/her argument

Theorists such as Dicey consider Parliament to be supreme. The European Convention on Human Rights now means that Parliament cannot pass any law that is against the Human Rights Act and so this means that Parliament is no longer supreme. However, Parliament was the body that enacted the Human Rights Act and it can repeal the Act and so Parliament is still supreme in the sense that it has only temporarily limited its power.

Correct, although the student could have made a reference to the case of *Thorburn* and the concept of constitutional statutes for added marks. But, the student needed to provide evidence in support of this point. How did the student know that this is true? S/he should have provided a footnote to the academic source

In conclusion, parliamentary sovereignty may exist as Parliament can repeal the ECA 1972 and the HRA 1998, but the power of Parliament to legislate has been limited by joining Europe and the ECHR and therefore Dicey's theory of sovereignty is not totally correct.

> This does sum up the crux of the essay, but it is a little brief. It may have been better to distinguish between the legal reality and the political reality of supremacy and/or to point to the subtleties of the difference between delegation and loss of sovereignty and also the limits of areas covered by EC law and the ECHR. Plus the ECHR is a treaty and not a body. The sentence needed to refer to bodies or documents but not a combination of both

[418 words]

> Overall, this essay attempts to address the question, squarely. There are some serious errors of understanding in relation to the HRA 1998 and how the ECHR operates in the UK. These detract from some of the points that were relatively correct. The paragraph structure needs work so that the essay flows, and each argument is developed and concluded in a single paragraph. Some paragraphs do not end with a conclusion, others do not begin by setting out the point to be made but instead launch into the evidence. Some of the sentences need work to improve their style. There is a lack of evidence to support some of the points being made and a complete lack of references to sources used; this really pulled down the marks to be awarded. The conclusion was a little too brief.

The mark awarded was 45% for a short essay of about 500 words. This essay did attempt to address the subject matter of the question. There was application of some relevant material – reference was made to the EU and the ECA 1972 as well as the HRA 1998. Presentation was adequate; however, the language used was at times formal and at other times informal. The student appeared to be familiar with the subject, although there was some confusion surrounding the Human Rights Act 1998 and the European Convention on Human Rights.

The essay would have been greatly improved by the following:

- an introduction that addressed all the key issues in the title rather than purely sovereignty and the EU;
- a proper series of paragraphs rather than unfinished paragraphs;
- a paragraph defining the main issue in the question – parliamentary sovereignty;
- more evidence to back up the points being made;
- conclusions at the end of each paragraph to round off the issue and to explain its relevance to the question;
- a reference to the text from which the student has taken the example about 'smoking on the streets of Paris';

- a reference to the *Thorburn* case, sometimes known as the *Metric Martyrs* case, rather than purely to the facts of the case. The legal issue in the case needed to be discussed rather than the background facts;
- full case citations and full citations of Acts of Parliament including the year of enactment;
- more formal language;
- proofreading for obvious errors;
- some of the law was correct, but some was muddled – the ECHR and the HRA 1998 were not correctly described.

The essay, if properly written and structured, would probably have achieved a mark in the 50–59% range, although without more evidence to back up the points being made, it would have been unlikely to have been awarded a mark of 60% or above.

CHAPTER 2: TEST YOUR KNOWLEDGE OF ESSAY WRITING

It has been suggested that the British Parliament was once supreme, but that its supremacy has been eroded as a result of Britain's membership of the EU and its signature of the European Convention on Human Rights. In order to examine this proposition it is necessary to consider the definition of parliamentary supremacy and differing theories of supremacy. The essay will consider evidence in respect of Britain's membership of the EU and the extent to which that affects Parliamentary supremacy. The essay will also consider Britain's signature of the European Convention of Human Rights in the same light.

There is evidence to suggest that as a result of Britain's membership of the EU, Parliament is no longer supreme. Britain joined the European Community and by passing the European Communities Act 1972, gave effect to EC law within our domestic jurisdiction. Section 2(1) states that 'All such rights, powers, liabilities, obligations and restrictions from time to time created or arising by or under the Treaties . . . as . . . are without further enactment to be given legal effect or used in the United Kingdom shall be recognised and available in law, and be enforced . . .' This primacy of European Community law was evidenced in the case of *R v. Secretary of State for Transport ex p. Factortame (No. 2)* (1991) in which EC law was applied in that case even though this meant that sections of the Merchant Shipping Act 1988 had to be disapplied as they directly contradicted EC law.[1] Parliament had passed the Act subsequent to the Euro-

---

1 Barnett, H. *Constitutional and Administrative Law* 7th edn (London: Routledge-Cavendish, 2008) p 133.

pean legislation and thus there could be no question that the will of Parliament was to legislate in contravention of Community law. This suggests that Parliamentary supremacy has been eroded, as the courts will not apply British law that contravenes directly applicable EC law.

CHAPTER 6: TEST YOUR UNDERSTANDING OF REFERENCING: CITING OTHERS' WORK

1 'Under any constitution – whether written or unwritten – there must be a source of ultimate authority: one supreme power over and above all other power in the state.'[2]

2 Barnett highlights Dicey's view that parliamentary sovereignty as one of the organising theories of our constitution and its nature and characteristics provoke debate amongst theoreticians of all descriptions.[3] She considers that international lawyers focus on state sovereignty in international terms, whereas political scientists consider sovereignty in the light of political governance. Lawyers examine sovereignty, perhaps unsurprisingly, from a legal standpoint, identifying the nature of legislative power within the State.[4]

3 'The requirement of obedience to law is strict: and yet there are limits:

If the Sovereign command a man (though justly condemned) to kill, wound, or mayme himselfe; or not to resist those that assault him; or to abstain from the use of food, ayre, medicine, or any other thing, without which he cannot live; yet hath that man the Liberty to disobey.'[5]

Or

'The requirement of obedience to law is strict: and yet there are limits: "If the Soveraign command a man (though justly condemned)

---

2 Barnett, H. *Constitutional and Administrative Law* 7th edn (London: Routledge-Cavendish, 2008) p 133.

3 Dicey, A.V. *Introduction to the Study of the Law of the Constitution* 10th edn (London: Palgrave Macmillan, 1885) p 39 as cited by Barnett, H. *Constitutional and Administrative Law* 7th edn (London: Routledge-Cavendish, 2008) pp 133–4.

4 Barnett, H. *Constitutional and Administrative Law* 7th edn (London: Routledge-Cavendish, 2008) pp 133–4.

5 Hobbes, T. *The Leviathan* (1651) (London: J.M. Dent, 1973) as cited in Barnett, H. *Constitutional and Administrative Law* 7th edn (London: Routledge-Cavendish, 2008) pp 134–5.

to kill, wound, or mayme himselfe; or not to resist those that assault him; or to abstain from the use of food, ayre, medicine, or any other thing, without which he cannot live; yet hath that man the Liberty to disobey." [6]

Some points to note for guidance:

- You should not simply put quotation marks round the extracts and consider that to be an appropriate answer. This will not be paraphrasing, but rather a direct quote.
- If you are paraphrasing someone else's words, then try to use your own words as far as possible. It is usually easiest to do this by reading a passage, then putting it to one side, so that you may then summarise the points in your own words, rather than trying to use your own words while still looking at the original text. Please do check to see whether you have simply changed round the word order in a sentence, but otherwise copied Barnett's work.
- The paragraphs should be read and analysed and your paragraph should contain a summary of the key concepts.
- Referencing is difficult if you are referencing someone else's source and they have not included a full citation. There are two schools of thought on this: 1) use the reference that the author put in her own footnote; and 2) look up the full reference and put that in your footnote before the 'as cited in' part of your footnote. Barnett lists full citations in the bibliography at the back of her book, so it has been included in the footnotes here.
- Check that you have fully referenced Barnett's work in footnotes, for both paraphrased and quoted passages.

REFERENCING EXERCISE 2: FULL AND ACCURATE REFERENCING

Source 1:

Murphy, T, 'Cosmopolitan Feminism: Towards a Critical Reappraisal of the Late Modern British State' in Millns, S and Whitty, N (eds) *Feminist Perspectives on Public Law* (London: Cavendish Publishing, 1999) pp 19–40.

---

6 Id.

Or

Murphy, T, 'Cosmopolitan Feminism: Towards a Critical Reappraisal of the Late Modern British State' in Millns, S and Whitty, N (eds) *Feminist Perspectives on Public Law*, 1999, London: Cavendish Publishing pp 19–40.

Or

Murphy, T, (1999) 'Cosmopolitan Feminism: Towards a Critical Reappraisal of the Late Modern British State' in Millns, S and Whitty, N (eds) *Feminist Perspectives on Public Law* London: Cavendish Publishing pp 19–40.

You may choose to put full stops after the authors' initials and after the abbreviation for pages (p. or pp.).

Source 2:

Barnett, H. *Constitutional and Administrative Law* 7th edn (London: Routledge-Cavendish, 2008).

Or

Barnett, H *Constitutional and Administrative Law* 7th edn, 2008, London: Routledge-Cavendish.

Or

Barnett, H (2008) *Constitutional and Administrative Law* 7th edn (London: Routledge-Cavendish).

CHAPTER 7:   TESTING YOUR UNDERSTANDING OF STYLE ISSUES

1 *'It could be considered that Parliamentary supremacy has been eroded, and some may suggest lost entirely, as a result of Britain joining the European Community.'*

This sentence should be followed with a discussion of the point, including evidence to back up the assertions.

2 *'The <u>Factortame (No. 2)</u> case provided evidence of the way in which European law is interpreted by the domestic courts where there is a conflict between European law and an Act of Parliament. In that instance, the House of Lords granted interim relief to the plaintiffs pending a decision by the European Court of Justice on the meaning and the impact of the European provision. Following the ruling of the European Court of Justice it is clear that in a situation where there is a direct conflict*

between such an EU provision and an Act of Parliament, the British courts are required to give precedence to the European legislation and, if necessary, to apply this in place of the British Act of Parliament.'

This sentence would need to be followed with evidence pointing to the relevant judgment within *Factortame (No. 2)*, to back up this assertion.

3 *'It could be suggested that the Human Rights Act 1998 has become semi-entrenched within the British Constitution, if one were to believe that the public would not tolerate any attempt to repeal the Act, and thus that Parliament would not readily repeal the Act.'*

The writer would need to provide evidence to back up this assertion.

BIBLIOGRAPHY

Bradney, A., Cownie, F., Masson, J., Neal, A. and Newell, D. *How to Study Law* 5th edn (London: Sweet and Maxwell, 2005) – Part Two is particularly good on research and on how to read and to use cases and statutes.

Clinch, P. *Using a Law Library: A Student's Guide to Legal Research Skills* 2nd edn (London: Blackstone Press, 2001) – A very good guide to making the most of your library and your research tools.

Haigh, R. *Legal English* 2nd edn (London: Routledge-Cavendish, 2009).

Hanson, S. *Legal Method, Skills and Reasoning* 3rd edn (London: Routledge-Cavendish, 2009) – Strong on all aspects of legal method; a particular favourite with students who learn through diagrams.

Holland, J.A. and Webb, J.S. *Learning Legal Rules* 6th edn (Oxford: OUP, 2006) – Particularly good on legal method, on reading the law and on law, fact and language.

Knowles, J. and Thomas, P. *Knowles and Thomas: Effective Legal Research* 5th edn (London: Sweet & Maxwell Ltd, 2006) – A comprehensive legal research guide that addresses print and online sources, and domestic and EC law.

McVea, H. and Cumper, P. *Exam Skills for Law Students* 2nd edn (Oxford: OUP, 2006) – Just as the title suggests, this book takes you through exam skills in detail.

Murray, R. *How to Write a Thesis* 2nd edn (Maidenhead: Open UP, 2006) – A great book for students who are undertaking dissertations or other forms of extended writing.

Slapper, G. and Kelly, D. *Questions and Answers on the English Legal System 2009–2010* (London: Routledge-Cavendish, 2009) – A useful guide to help you with revision for any English legal system exam. It provides excellent examples of essay and problem question answers.

Slapper, G. and Kelly, D. *The English Legal System* 10th edn (London:

Routledge-Cavendish, 2009) – A strong, annually updated textbook that will provide background and evidence in relation to most aspects of the English legal system (ELS). This may be a useful starting point for essays that involved ELS themes. Visit the book's useful companion website at www.routledge.com/textbooks/9780415480963, particularly for its Legal Skills Guides on skills including legal writing and mooting.

Strong, S. *How to Write Law Essays and Exams* 2nd edn (Oxford: OUP, 2006) – This is a more detailed look at legal writing and provides a comprehensive account of the CLEO writing system to assist with essays and exam writing in law.

INDEX